Berklee Practice Method

DRUM SET

Get Your Band Together

RON SAVAGE
CASEY SCHEUERELL
and the
Berklee Faculty

T0048526

Berklee Press

Director: Dave Kusek
Managing Editor: Debbie Cavalier
Marketing Manager: Ola Frank
Sr. Writer/Editor: Jonathan Feist
Writer/Editor: Susan Gedutis
Product Manager: Ilene Altman

ISBN 978-0-634-00652-5

berklee press

1140 Boylston Street
Boston, MA 02215-3693 USA
(617) 747-2146

Visit Berklee Press Online at
www.berkleepress.com

DISTRIBUTED BY

HAL•LEONARD®
CORPORATION
7777 W. BLUEMOUND RD. P.O. BOX 13819
MILWAUKEE, WISCONSIN 53213

Visit Hal Leonard Online at
www.halleonard.com

DESIGN TEAM

Matt Marvuglio	Curriculum Editor
	Dean of the Professional Performance Division
Jonathan Feist	Series Editor
	Senior Writer/Editor, Berklee Press

Rich Appleman	Chair of the Bass Department
Larry Baione	Chair of the Guitar Department
Jeff Galindo	Assistant Professor of Brass
Matt Glaser	Chair of the String Department
Russell Hoffmann	Assistant Professor of Piano
Charles Lewis	Associate Professor of Brass
Jim Odgren	Academic Advising Coordinator
Tiger Okoshi	Assistant Professor of Brass
Bill Pierce	Chair of the Woodwind Department
Tom Plsek	Chair of the Brass Department
Mimi Rabson	Assistant Professor of Strings
John Repucci	Assistant Chair of the Bass Department
Ed Saindon	Assistant Professor of Percussion
Ron Savage	Chair of the Ensemble Department
Casey Scheuerell	Associate Professor of Percussion
Paul Schmeling	Chair of the Piano Department
Jan Shapiro	Chair of the Voice Department

The Band

Rich Appleman, Bass
Larry Baione, Guitar
Jim Odgren, Alto Sax
Casey Scheuerell, Drums
Paul Schmeling, Keyboard

Music composed by Matt Marvuglio

Contents

CD Tracks

Chapter I. Playing Rock ("Sweet")

CD 1. "Sweet" Full Band

CD 2. "Sweet" Bass and Drums (one chorus)

CD 3. "Sweet" Keyboard and Drums (one chorus)

CD 4. "Sweet" You're the Drummer

CD 5. "Sweet" Call/Response 1

CD 6. "Sweet" Call/Response 2

Chapter II. Playing Blues ("Do It Now")

CD 7. "Do It Now" Full Band

CD 8. "Do It Now" You're the Drummer

CD 9. "Do It Now" Call/Response 1

CD 10. "Do It Now" Call/Response 2

Chapter III. Playing Shuffle Blues ("I Just Wanna Be With You")

CD 11. "I Just Wanna Be With You" Full Band

CD 12. "I Just Wanna Be With You" You're the Drummer

CD 13. "I Just Wanna Be With You" Call/Response 1

CD 14. "I Just Wanna Be With You" Call/Response 2

Chapter IV. Playing Funk ("Leave Me Alone")

CD 15. "Leave Me Alone" Full Band

CD 16. "Leave Me Alone" You're the Drummer

CD 17. "Leave Me Alone" Call/Response 1

CD 18. "Leave Me Alone" Call/Response 2

Foreword

Berklee College of Music has been training musicians for over fifty years. Our graduates go onto successful careers in the music business, and many have found their way to the very top of the industry, producing hit records, receiving the highest awards, and sharing their music with millions of people.

An important reason why Berklee is so successful is that our curriculum stresses the practical application of musical principles. Our students spend a lot of time playing together in bands. When you play with other musicians, you learn things that are impossible to learn in any other way. Teachers are invaluable, practicing by yourself is critical, but performing in a band is the most valuable experience of all. That's what is so special about this series: it gives you the theory you need, but also prepares you to play in a band.

The goal of the *Berklee Practice Method* is to present some of Berklee's teaching strategies in book and audio form. The chairs of each of our instrumental departments—guitar, bass, keyboard, percussion, woodwind, brass, string, and voice—have gotten together and discussed the best ways to teach you how to play in a band. They teamed with some of our best faculty and produced a set of books with play-along audio tracks that uniquely prepares its readers to play with other musicians.

Students who want to study at Berklee come from a variety of backgrounds. Some have great technique, but have never improvised. Some have incredible ears, but need more work on their reading skills. Some have a very creative, intuitive sense of music, but their technical skills aren't strong enough, yet, to articulate their ideas.

The *Berklee Practice Method* teaches many of these different aspects of musicianship. It is the material that our faculty wishes all Berklee freshmen could master before arriving on our doorstep.

When you work through this book, don't just read it. You've got to play through every example, along with the recording. Better yet, play them with your own band.

Playing music with other people is how you will learn the most. This series will help you master the skills you need to become a creative, expressive, and supportive musician that anyone would want to have in their band.

Gary Burton
Executive Vice President,
Berklee College of Music

Preface

Thank you for choosing the *Berklee Practice Method* for drums. This book/CD package, developed by the faculty of Berklee College of Music, is part of the *Berklee Practice Method* series—the instrumental method that teaches how to play in a band.

The recording included with this method provides an instant band you can play along with, featuring great players from Berklee's performance faculty. Each tune has exercises and practice tracks that will help prepare you to play it. Rock, blues, and funk are just some of the styles you will perform.

The lessons in this book will guide you through basic rhythms, beats, and subdivisions. You'll learn about song forms and techniques for how to play in a band. It is intended for drummers who are just beginning to take lessons with their teacher, though drummers learning on their own will also find it invaluable.

Most important, you will learn the skills you need to play drums in a band. Play along with the recording, and play with your friends. This series coordinates methods for many different instruments, and all are based on the same tunes, in the same keys. If you know a guitarist, bass player, keyboardist, etc., have them pick up the *Berklee Practice Method* for their own instruments, and then you can jam together.

Work hard, make music, have fun!

Ron Savage
Chair of the Ensemble Department
Berklee College of Music

Casey Scheuerell
Associate Professor of Percussion
Berklee College of Music

Basics

Before you start chapter 1, you should understand the following topics.

PARTS OF A DRUM SET

SETTING UP

This is a common setup. You may not have all these drums. A kit with just bass drum, snare, ride cymbal, and hi-hat is fine for most styles of music.

Right-Handed Setup

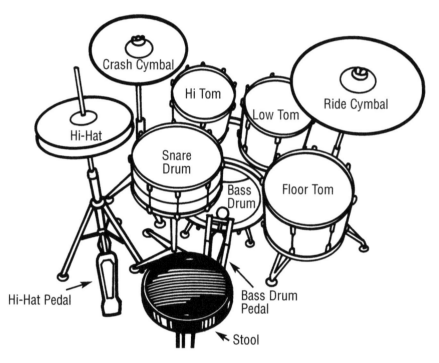

Left-Handed Setup

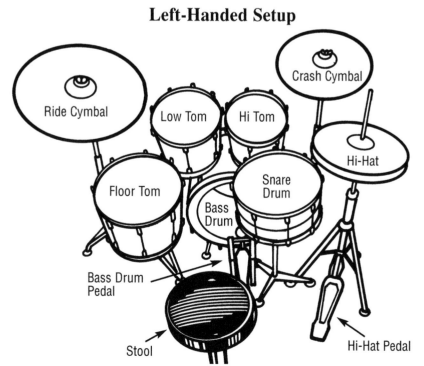

If you are left-handed, you might reverse the drums and cymbals shown in the right-handed setup.

PLAYING POSITION

When you play the drum set, sit up straight, but be relaxed and comfortable. Keep a mirror where you practice, and check your posture frequently.

HAND POSITION

There are two basic grips: matched and traditional. For most drum set playing, you'll probably use a matched grip.

Matched Grip

Traditional Grip

NOTATION

Notes are written on a staff.

RHYTHMS

These are the basic rhythms. Beats are numbered below the staff.

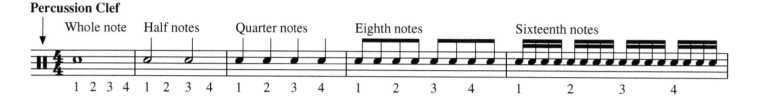

Percussion Clef

Whole note   Half notes   Quarter notes   Eighth notes   Sixteenth notes

Connect notes using a tie. The first note is held for a total of six beats.

Extend a note's rhythmic value by using a dot. A dot increases the value by one half.

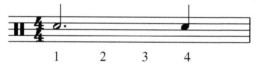

Triplets squeeze three even attacks into the space of one quarter-note beat.

INSTRUMENTS

In this book, drums are notated with a dot notehead (●) and cymbals are notated with an x notehead (x).

If the stem goes up, then the drum or cymbal is played with your hands (sticks). If the stem goes down, it is played with your feet. Each drum has a unique position on the staff:

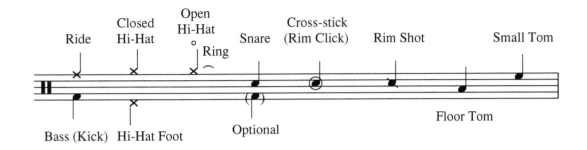

RHYTHMIC NOTATION

Music that just shows rhythms may be written in rhythmic notation. This is common in clapping exercises. The stems are the same, but the noteheads are different.

MEASURES

Groups of beats are divided into measures. Measure lengths are shown with *time signatures.*
This measure is in $\frac{4}{4}$ time—there are four quarter notes in the measure.

In $\frac{12}{8}$ time, there are twelve eighth notes per measure.

RUDIMENTS

All drumming, regardless of the style or approach, is made up of sticking patterns called *rudiments*.

Each rudiment can be viewed as a specific building block for drumming and therefore used in any number of variations.

The rudiments are the ABCs of drumming and when practiced properly, will help you improve your control of the sticks, evenness between hands, dynamics, and sense of timing.

PRACTICE TIPS

Throughout this book, you will learn rudiments. Here are some tips for making rudimental practice productive.

1. Always practice rudiments slowly and steadily until the sticking feels natural.

2. When the sticking feels natural, gradually increase the speed until you reach your maximum point of control, then gradually slow down until you reach the original tempo.

3. Grace notes should always be played one inch from the drum. Full strokes should be played six inches from the drum. Accented strokes should be played eight inches from the drum.

4. Strive for evenness in motion and sound for all full strokes.

Now, let's play!

"Sweet" is a *rock* tune. Rock started in the 1960s and has roots in blues, swing, r&b, and rock 'n' roll. There are many different styles of rock. To hear more rock, listen to artists such as Rage Against the Machine, Melissa Etheridge, Korn, Paula Cole, Bjork, Tori Amos, Primus, Jimi Hendrix, and Led Zeppelin.

LESSON 1
TECHNIQUE/THEORY

LISTEN **1** **PLAY**

Listen to "Sweet" on the recording, and then play along.

LEARNING THE BEAT

To learn the beat, follow these three steps:

    1. Start with the hi-hat or ride cymbal.
    2. Add the snare drum.
    3. Add the bass drum.

The tune "Sweet" has two parts. Here is the beat for the first part:

In the second part, the hi-hat part moves to the ride cymbal:

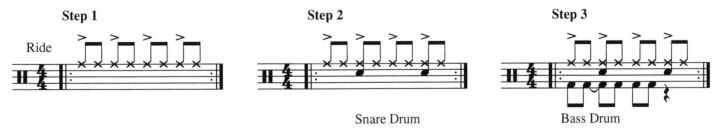

Play along with the recording and match the drummer. Keep the beat steady. Remember, the drummer is responsible for keeping everyone true to the time.

ROCK TECHNIQUE

When you play the beat to "Sweet," use a matched grip. Make sure that you are relaxed, and that your posture is good. Even when you play driving rock beats like this, stay relaxed. It will help you move more freely and have more stamina.

In rock playing, more important than sheer volume is the relative dynamics between each of your drums and cymbals. A big sound is not necessarily a loud sound. The bass drum and snare should be relatively loud, and the hi-hat and ride should be softer.

LESSON 2
LEARNING THE GROOVE

WHAT IS A GROOVE?

A *groove* is a combination of musical patterns in which everyone in the band feels and plays to a common pulse. This creates a sense of unity and momentum. The *rhythm section* (usually drums, bass, guitar, and keyboard) lays down the groove's dynamic and rhythmic feel. A singer or soloist also contributes to the groove and performs the melody based on this feel.

Listen to "Sweet." As is common in hard rock, the groove to "Sweet" has a strong, clear pulse, and a loud, forceful sound. The drums play a heavy, repetitive beat. The bass outlines the harmonic structure. The guitar and keyboards play chords. Everyone uses the same rhythms, though often at different times. This makes the whole band sound like one unit, or *hooked up* with the groove.

HOOKING UP

In lesson 1, you hooked into a groove. As you heard, the drummer's job in a groove is to keep time for the band.

Listen to "Sweet" and focus on the bass drum and bass guitar. Hear where their parts connect, or *hook up*. When does the bass play on the beat and when does it play on a subdivision of the beat? What about the guitar and keyboard?

Play your bass drum part along with the recording and listen for the bass guitar.

Keep playing the bass drum, and clap the bass guitar rhythms. Notice when they play simultaneously:

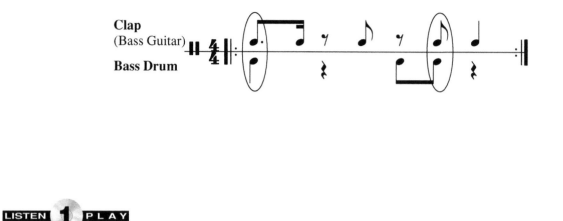

LISTEN 1 PLAY

Try clapping the keyboard and guitar parts along with the bass drum. As you can see, the rhythms of every part come from the drum beat. If you play your part steadily and accurately, you will help your whole band to hook up to the groove.

ROCK FEELS

The smallest beat subdivision you have been playing is the eighth note, so you could say that this beat has an *eighth-note feel*. Many rock beats have an eighth-note feel, but sometimes, they have a *sixteenth-note feel*. You could also use a beat with a sixteenth-note feel on this tune.

LESSON 3
IMPROVISATION

Improvisation means creating your part as you play. Drum parts are often partially improvised, with variations to the beat, fills, and even longer drum solos. Though an improvised solo may seem spontaneous to the audience, there is a lot of preparation that comes before a musician plays it. There are two things you must know before you start improvising: when you should play, and what rhythms will sound good. The first step is to know the tune.

FORM

When you are preparing to play a tune, start by learning how it is organized. You have to know where you are in the music so that your beat will sound good with what the other instruments are playing. This will also help you keep your place—especially when you are accompanying a soloist's improvisation, and nobody is playing the written melody.

Listen to "Sweet" and follow the saxophone. After an introduction, the sax plays the melody. Then, it improvises a solo. Finally, it plays the melody again.

During the improvised solo, you can still feel the written melody. That's because the improvisation follows the same chords as the written melody. This repeating chord pattern is the same throughout the entire tune, and is called the song's *form*—its plan or structure.

A common way to show this organization is with a *chord chart*. Chord charts don't show rhythm or pitch, only measures and chord symbols, which are used by the rest of the band to know what notes to play. Each symbol (letter, often with a dash or number) represents a chord. By following the chord symbols and listening to the other musicians, you can keep your place in the form. The slash marks (/ / / /) mean "play in time."

The chord chart makes it easy to see that the form of "Sweet' is sixteen measures long. It has two primary musical ideas: the first eight measures present the first idea (idea "A"), with the **E– A E–** chord patterns played by the rest of the band. The second eight measures present the second idea (idea "B'), with the **A– D A– D** patterns. This form can be described simply as "AB" or "AB form." These letters help us remember the form, freeing us from having to read while we're performing.

One complete repetition of this form is called a *chorus*. A chorus can feature the written melody, in which case it is called the *head*, or it can feature just the chord structure, supporting an improvisation. (The word *chorus* is also used to mean a song section that is alternated with varying verses. In this book, however, the word "chorus" is only used to mean "once through the form.")

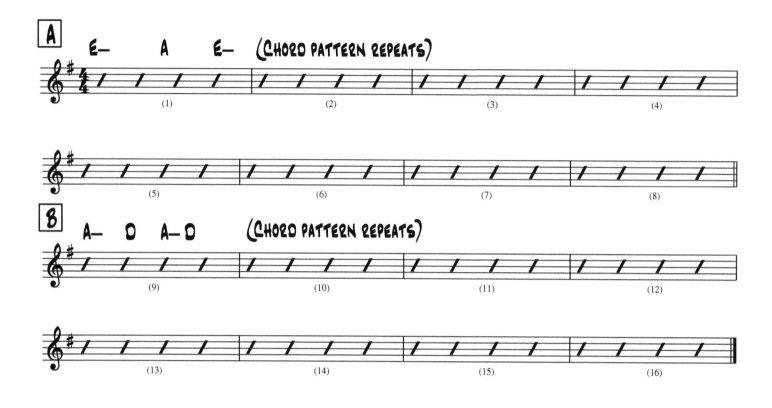

FOLLOWING THE CHORDS

Listen to just the drums and keyboard. Follow the chord chart and notice when the keyboard changes chords.

KEEPING THE FORM

LISTEN **1** PLAY

One of your primary responsibilities as a drummer is to help the band keep a sense of form. Listen to "Sweet," count the measures, and follow the bass and keyboard as they change chords. The bass usually plays the bottom note of a new chord, as soon as that chord comes in. Pay close attention to the bass on the first beat of each measure. New chords are often introduced on beat 1, especially at the downbeat of new song sections. Try changing the beat slightly to fit each section of the tune.

SING THE BASS

LISTEN 1 PLAY

Listen to "Sweet," and sing along with the bass part on the downbeat of each measure. Notice when it moves to the new chord pattern (measure 9).

ARRANGEMENT

Your band can choose how many choruses you want to play, and create your own *arrangement* of "Sweet." The number of choruses depends on how many players will improvise when you perform the tune. On the recorded performance of "Sweet," only one player solos (the sax), playing for two choruses. Often, several members of the band will take turns playing choruses of improvised solos. A solo can be one or two choruses, or even more.

On the recording, the same basic arrangement is used for all the tunes: the head, an improvised sax solo, and then the head again. There are often short introductions and endings as well.

LISTEN 1 PLAY

Listen to "Sweet" and follow the arrangement. This is the arrangement for "Sweet" played on the recording:

INTRO	HEAD	SAX SOLO: 2x	HEAD	ENDING
4 MEASURES	1 CHORUS = 16 MEASURES	1 CHORUS = 16 MEASURES	1 CHORUS = 16 MEASURES	2 MEASURES

When you play "Sweet" with your band, you can play your own arrangement, adding extra solo choruses, different endings, or other changes.

SHAPING THE ARRANGEMENT

When soloists improvise, they must know where they are in the form at all times so that their part hooks up with the rest of the band. The drummer can help the band keep a sense of form and arrangement by playing small *fills* after every group of four and eight measures. Fills are short, often improvised drum flourishes, usually occurring on the last few beats of a phrase and often signaling a section change. Then, at the start of a new section, you can play a different beat or variation of the same beat.

VARIATIONS

LISTEN **4** PLAY

Use the three-step system (see lesson 1) to practice these rock beats. When you can play them comfortably, practice them along with the recording.

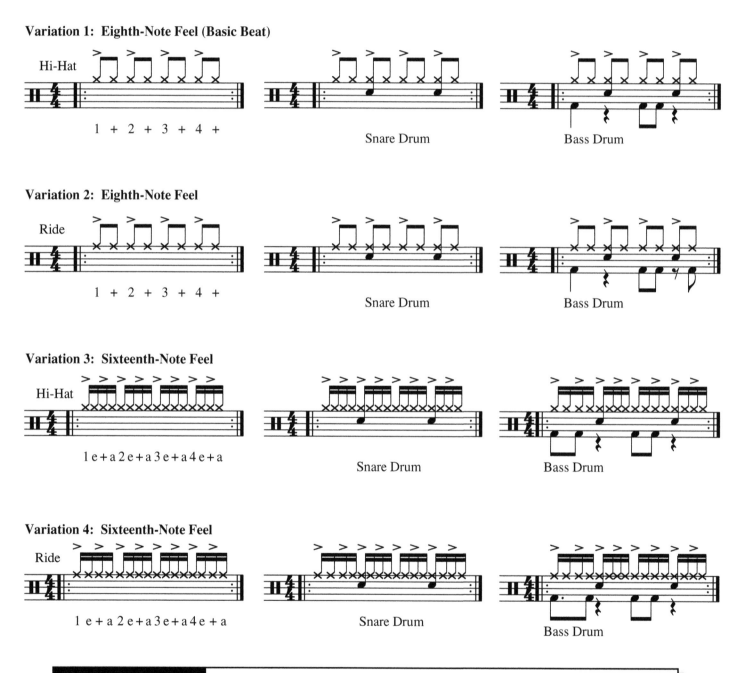

Variation 1: Eighth-Note Feel (Basic Beat)

Hi-Hat

1 + 2 + 3 + 4 +

Snare Drum

Bass Drum

Variation 2: Eighth-Note Feel

Ride

1 + 2 + 3 + 4 +

Snare Drum

Bass Drum

Variation 3: Sixteenth-Note Feel

Hi-Hat

1 e + a 2 e + a 3 e + a 4 e + a

Snare Drum

Bass Drum

Variation 4: Sixteenth-Note Feel

Ride

1 e + a 2 e + a 3 e + a 4 e + a

Snare Drum

Bass Drum

PRACTICE TIP

Practice slowly at first. When you can perform the beat correctly, increase the tempo, and keep increasing it gradually until you are at the same tempo as the recording. Musicians—even pros at the highest levels—do this all the time, behind the scenes. It's a great way of playing rhythms very accurately, and helps you hook up tightly with your band.

CALL AND RESPONSE

Listen to each beat and then echo it exactly. Follow the form and try to capture the rhythmic quality of the beat being played. Slashes ("/") in measures marked "play" mean that you should play during those measures. Listen carefully and hook up with the groove.

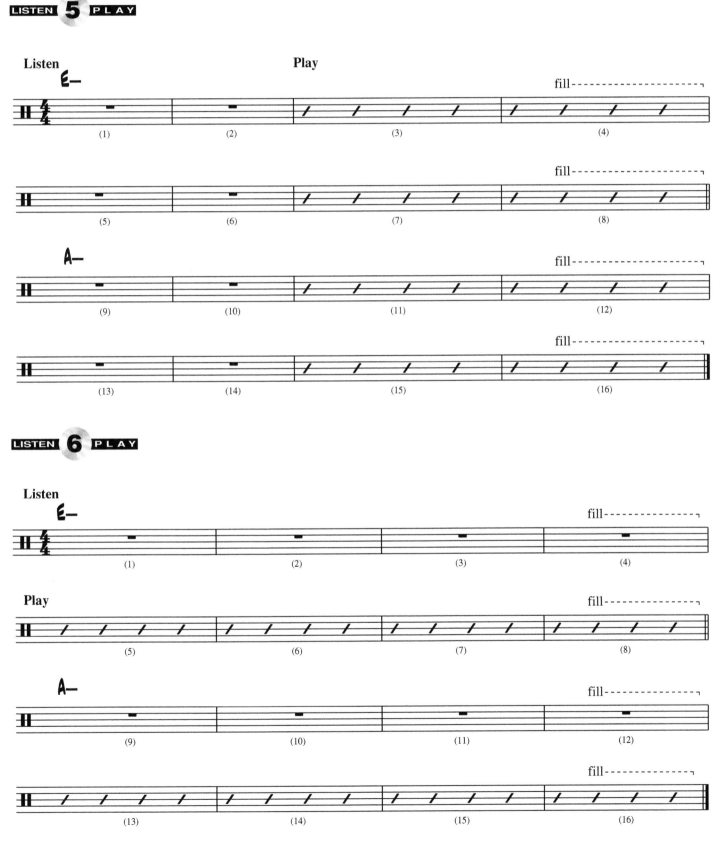

 **LISTEN 5,6 PLAY**

Play the same track again. This time, instead of echoing an exact response, answer them with your own improvised fill. Imitate the sound and rhythmic feel of each one, and only use rhythms typical of the rock style.

PERFORMANCE TIP

In the call and response exercise, you played a fill every few measures. When you are actually performing a tune, use fills more sparingly. Fills work well for signaling section changes, or on new choruses, but most of the time, you should keep a regular beat. If you wait longer, and then play longer fills, it is a lot more effective than playing fills too often.

CREATE YOUR OWN

 **LISTEN 4 PLAY**

Create your own drum part using any of the beats and fills you just played, and practice your part along with the recording. Keep one consistent beat through each section of the song and add fills at the end of each section. Try different beat variations for each section as the song progresses.

PLAY IN A BAND TIP

When playing in a band, listen to the other players' parts and try to create a musical conversation. This makes playing much more fun, and more musical too. When you are improvising a beat or fill, listen to what the other instruments are playing. They will suggest many ideas that you can use in your beats and fills, and you will inspire

---

LESSON 4
READING

When you play in a band, sometimes you will get a drum part for the tune that shows exactly what you should play. Other times, you will get a lead sheet, giving you more freedom to create your own part. You should be able to play from either one.

DRUM PART

On the next page is the drum part to "Sweet." Above the drum line are chord symbols. Some drum parts show chord symbols, but often they do not.

INTRO	Introduction. The drum part begins with an introduction, which is made up of four measures of the B section.
HARD ROCK	Style indication. This tune is hard rock, and you should play it in that style: heavy bass drum and snare, strong beat, sixteenth-note feel, and other elements typical of that hard-edged sound.
♩ = 86	Metronome marking. This tells you how fast you should play this tune. If you have a metronome, set it to 86, and play "Sweet" at that tempo.
‖: :‖	Repeat signs. Play the music between these signs twice (or more).
[A]	Rehearsal letter. These are different than form letters, which you saw in lesson 3. These letters help you when you are practicing with other musicians because everyone's parts have the same letters marked at the same places.
[A9]	Rehearsal letter with measure number. These mark different areas within a chorus. Again, this can be helpful during rehearsals.
AFTER SOLOS, REPEAT TO ENDING	When the soloists are finished, play the head one more time, and then proceed to the measures marked "Ending."
ENDING	A final section that is added to the form. End the tune with these measures.

Play "Sweet" along with the recording. Follow the drum part.

Sweet

DRUM PART

BY MATT MARVUGLIO

LEAD SHEET

More commonly, you'll just get a *lead sheet*, which is the same for all instruments. A lead sheet has the melody and chords, and it shows the form of the tune. Sometimes, it will indicate the style of the tune. You can play any appropriate drum beat in that style, and add fills where you think they should go. Notice that there is no written introduction on this lead sheet. The introduction you hear in the recording is an interpretation of the lead sheet by that band. Your band should create your own unique arrangement.

LISTEN **4** PLAY

Play "Sweet" along with the recording. Follow the lead sheet, and use your own "hard rock" drum beats and fills.

SWEET

BY MATT MARVUGLIO

PLAY IN A BAND TIP
While you play, follow the lead sheet. It will help you keep your place in the form.

MEMORIZE

LISTEN **4** PLAY

Memorize your drum part to "Sweet," choosing fills where necessary. Performing is the best practice, so get together with other musicians and learn these tunes with your own band.

"Summary" shows everything you need to play "Sweet." Memorizing it will help you memorize the tune.

SUMMARY

FORM
16-Bar AB
(1 Chorus = 16 Bars)
A: 8 M.
B: 8 M.

ARRANGEMENT
Intro: 4 M.
1 Chorus Melody
2 Chorus Solo
1 Chorus Melody
End: 2 M.

BEATS

PLAY "SWEET" WITH YOUR OWN BAND!

CHAPTER I
DAILY PRACTICE ROUTINE

STICK CONTROL: QUARTER NOTES

1. Always keep a steady pulse. Practicing with a metronome or click track can be very helpful.
2. Strive for a consistent sound between your hands.
3. Play consistently on the same area of the drum or practice pad.
4. Focus on controlling the stick:
   a. With the fulcrum. The *fulcrum* is the balance point between the thumb and index finger.
   b. Using forearm motion to lift the stick up.
   c. Snapping your wrist to strike the drum.
5. Start these exercises slowly. Keep good posture, and relax your arms.

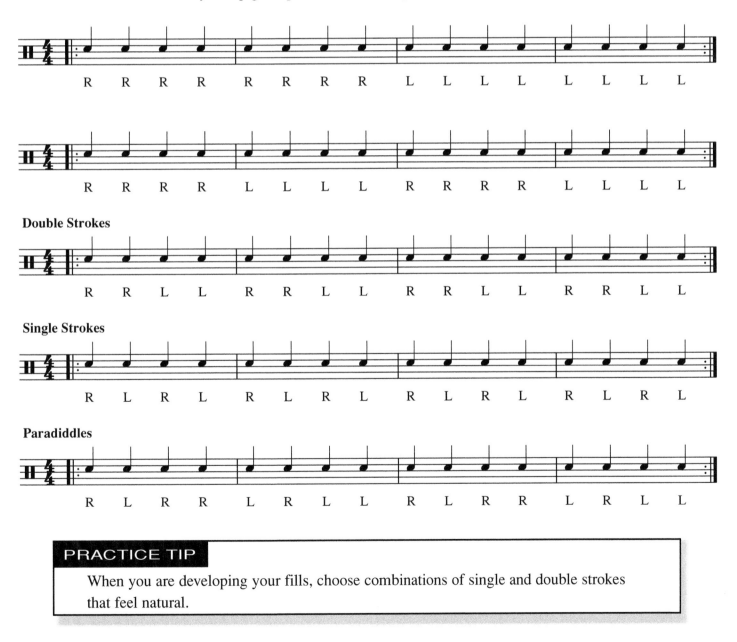

Double Strokes

Single Strokes

Paradiddles

PRACTICE TIP

When you are developing your fills, choose combinations of single and double strokes that feel natural.

"Do It Now" is a *blues* tune. Blues began in the late 1800s, and it has had a profound influence on American music styles, including rock, jazz, and soul. To hear more blues, listen to artists such as B.B. King, the Blues Brothers, Robben Ford, Bonnie Raitt, James Cotton, Albert King, and Paul Butterfield.

LESSON 5
TECHNIQUE/THEORY

LISTEN **7** PLAY

Listen to "Do It Now," and then play along with the recording. Try to match the drum part.

LEARNING THE BEAT

To learn the beat, follow these three steps:

1. Start with the hi-hat.
2. Add the snare drum.
3. Add the bass drum.

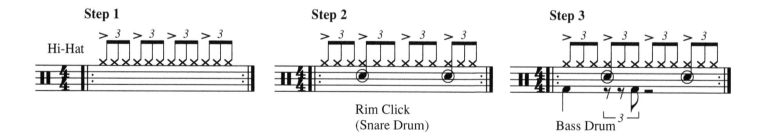

RIM CLICK

On the first verse of the recording, the snare drum is played with a *rim click* on beats 2 and 4. Rim clicks are played on the rim, and are common for lighter backbeats. It is a technique also used commonly in cha-cha and other Afro-Cuban rhythms.

To play a rim click:

1. Hold the stick backwards. Grasp it near the middle with your thumb and index finger. Your other fingers should rest on the stick comfortably. The drum stick tip should extend past your palm.

2. Place the stick on your snare drum with the tip about an inch from the rim. Rest your palm on the drum head.

3. Using the tip as a hinge, always connected to the head, tap the butt end of the stick against the rim, to get a "click" sound. By clicking different parts of the rim, you can get different pitches. Keep the tip at roughly the same spot. For this tune, find a spot on your rim that gives a high-pitched, cutting sound.

Rim clicks are often notated with a circled notehead (◉). They are most common on the snare drum.

LEARNING THE GROOVE

HOOKING UP TO A SHUFFLE

LISTEN **7** PLAY

Listen to "Do It Now." This groove has its roots in traditional r&b, gospel, and jazz. The feel is often called a 12/8 shuffle because of the twelve eighth notes in each bar (usually played on the ride cymbal or hi-hat).

Clap on every beat, and count even triplets:

Count	1	trip-let	2	trip-let	3	trip-let	4	trip-let
Clap	1		2		3		4	

The basic pulse (clap) is on the quarter note. However, each pulse also has an underlying triplet that divides the beat into three equal parts:

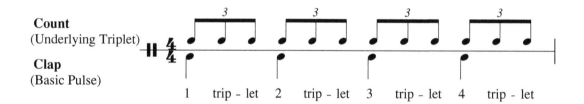

This triplet feel is part of what makes the beat a *shuffle*. While all shuffles don't include triplets on every single beat, the underlying triplet *feel* is always present. You might just play quarter notes in the hi-hat or ride. Practice this beat along with the recording.

LISTEN **8** PLAY

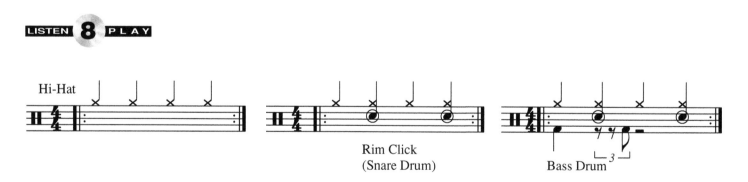

You could also play a *shuffle pattern*, with the first and third notes of the triplet. Practice this beat along with the recording.

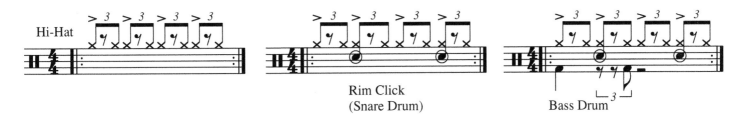

The exact beat on the recording is called a *12/8 shuffle* because it has all twelve triplet eighth notes in each measure. A slight accent on the first note of each triplet will settle the beat nicely.

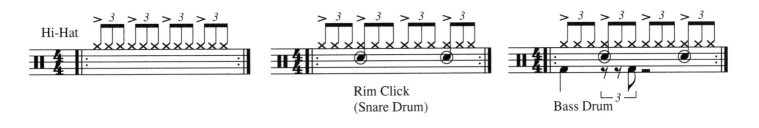

The triplet is a fundamental aspect of all swing and shuffle beats. Understanding and feeling the concept of *subdivisions* (dividing the pulse into smaller rhythms) will help you play many other kinds of grooves.

LEARNING "DO IT NOW"

"Do It Now" begins with the drums setting up the groove with two beats of triplets. This lets the listener know that a shuffle feel is coming. The other instruments play triplets in their parts as well. Where does the bass player play the triplet? Is it the same in every measure? What about the keyboard? Does it play all three beats of the triplet or just two? Where does the melody play triplets?

Listen to how the bass is locked in with the bass drum. On the downbeat of each bar, the bass begins in sync with the bass drum. It connects again at the "let" of beat 2. This hookup between the bass and drums creates the foundation of the groove. The guitar and keyboard are hooked into the hi-hat and snare parts.

LESSON 7
IMPROVISATION

FORM AND ARRANGEMENT: 12-BAR BLUES FORM

Listen to "Do It Now" and follow the form. The form of "Do It Now" is a *12-bar blues*. Its form is twelve measures long, with chords organized in this sequence:

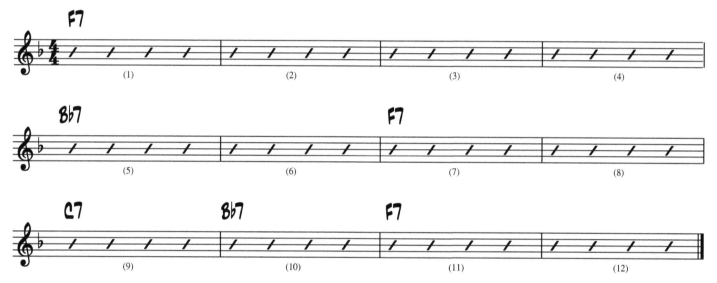

A 12-bar blues has three 4-bar phrases. It is common for the first two phrases in the melody to be similar and the third one to be different. This form is very common in many styles of music, including jazz, rock, and funk.

ARRANGEMENT

Listen to "Do It Now" and follow the arrangement. Listen to where the rest of the band switches chords. How many times does the form repeat at the head? How many times does it repeat during the solo? When does the drummer switch from hi-hat to ride cymbal?

"Do It Now" begins with two beats of triplets. This is called a *pickup*—a short introduction, less than a measure long, that leads to a strong downbeat. The arrangement played on the recording is:

PICKUP	HEAD: 2X	SAX SOLO: 2X	HEAD	ENDING
2 BEATS DRUMS	‖: 1 CHORUS = 12 MEASURES :‖	‖: 1 CHORUS = 12 MEASURES :‖	1 CHORUS = 12 MEASURES	4 MEASURES

The "X" symbol in "2X" means "play this section two times." This notation is common in lead sheets and drum charts.

PRACTICE TIP

When you listen to any music, figure out the arrangement. How long is the head? Is there an introduction or an ending? How many solo choruses does the band take?

SING THE BASS

LISTEN **7** PLAY

Listen again, follow the chord chart, and sing the bass note on the downbeat of each measure.

VARIATIONS

LISTEN **8** PLAY

Practice these variations. When you can play them comfortably, practice them along with the recording. Change your beat slightly in every chorus to create a more interesting drum part. Try going to the ride cymbal or to the bell of the cymbal. Use a rim click on the backbeat, embellish the bass drum, or use occasional cymbal crashes (don't overdo these). You can use beat variations to shape the form and help the rest of the band keep their place.

Hi-Hat Variations

Bass Drum Variations

CALL AND RESPONSE

1. Echo each phrase, exactly as you hear it.
2. Improvise an answer to each beat. Imitate its sound and rhythmic feel.

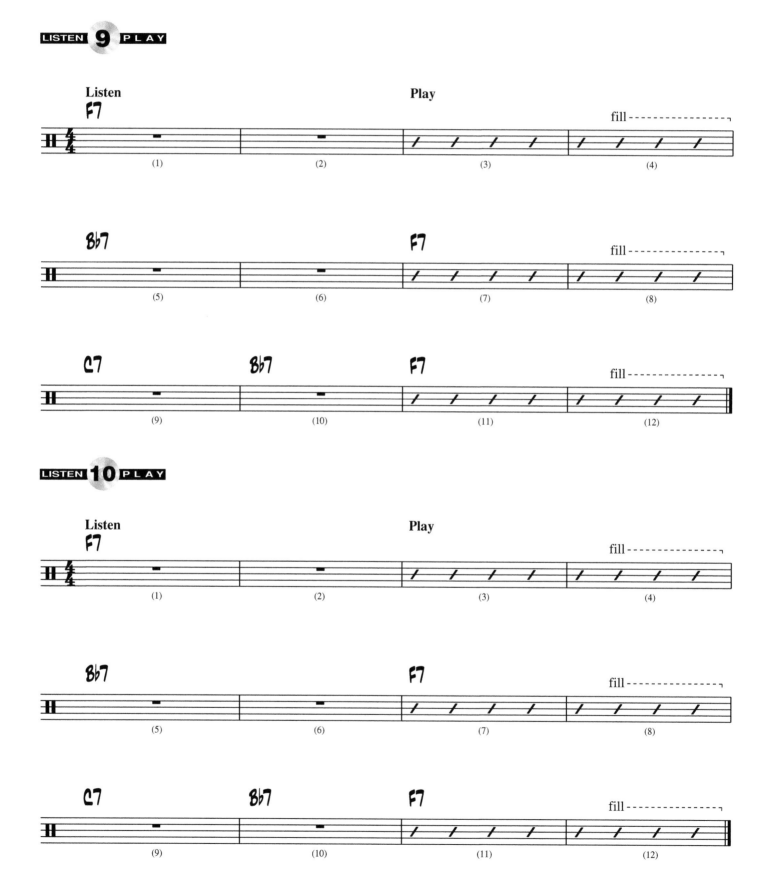

LESSON 8
READING

DRUM PART

This *chart* (written part) uses symbols and instructions that direct you to skip around the pages. When you get the hang of these symbols, you will see that they help reduce the number of written measures and make the chart easier to read quickly, at a glance. Sometimes, these directions are called the chart's *road map*.

𝄋	Sign. Later, there will be a direction (D.S., or "from the sign") telling you to jump to this symbol from another location in the music.
𝄌	Coda symbol. "Coda" is another word for "ending." On the last chorus, skip from the first coda symbol to the second coda symbol (at the end of the piece). This symbol may also have the words "To Coda," or other directions (such as "last time only"). Often, you will just see the coda symbol by itself.
D.S. AL 𝄌	From the sign (𝄋), and take the coda. Jump back to the sign (first measure, after the pickup), and play from there. When you reach the first coda symbol, skip ahead to the next coda symbol (at the end).
AFTER SOLOS	When all solo choruses are finished, follow this direction.
B	Different choruses may be marked with different letters. In this tune, the head is marked "A," and the improvisation choruses are marked "B."
SOLO	Solo chorus. Play this part when other musicians in the band improvise. When you play this tune with your own band, you might repeat this section several times, depending on how many people solo. When you solo, then obviously, you won't play this written part.
11 BARS GROOVE ∿∿∿∿	Continue your beat for eleven measures. Count each measure while you play to help you keep your place.

Play "Do It Now" along with the recording and follow the written drum part exactly. Even if you have it memorized already, follow along with the part as you play. Notice the written pickup and ending.

Do It Now
Drum Part

By Matt Marvuglio

24

LEAD SHEET

Now play "Do It Now" with the recording, but work from the lead sheet. Use your own drum beats.

Do It Now

BY MATT MARVUGLIO

MEMORIZE

Review the written drum part in lesson 8. Decide what beats you will play.

LISTEN **8** P L A Y

Memorize your part, and then play through the tune with the recording as if you were performing it live. Keep your place in the form, and don't stop, whatever happens.

> **PERFORMANCE TIP**
>
> If you make a mistake or get lost, keep your composure. Listen to the other instruments, hear what chords they are playing, and find your way back into the form.

Remember that keeping the groove is the most important thing. Simple drum beats can be very effective.

SUMMARY

FORM	ARRANGEMENT	BLUES 12/8 SHUFFLE BEAT
12-BAR BLUES	PICKUP: 2 BEATS DRUMS	
(1 CHORUS = 12 BARS)	2 CHORUS MELODY	
	2 CHORUS SOLO	
	1 CHORUS MELODY	
	END: 4 M.	

PLAY "DO IT NOW" WITH YOUR OWN BAND!

CHAPTER II
DAILY PRACTICE ROUTINE

CONTROLLING TRIPLETS

To make triplets sound natural, the first note should have a slight accent, and the other two should sound like follow-throughs of the first. Practice making each triplet group sound the same.

"1" The down stroke gives a natural accent to the first note of each triplet. The stroke gets its power from the wrist. Hold the stick firmly with your fingers.

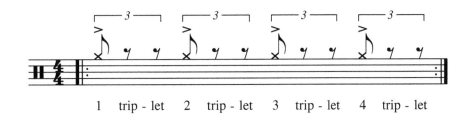

"trip-" Open your hand slightly, but hold the fulcrum firmly. The second note will come with very little effort. This is a "tap" stroke. It is softer, a natural reaction from the relaxed release of the previous "down" stroke.

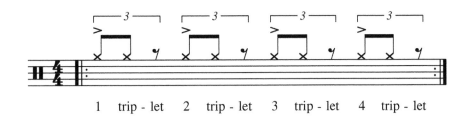

"let" The "up" stroke is also softer. It is created by slightly closing the hand as it is being raised by your wrist. Raising the stick after the hit will prepare you to start the cycle over again on the next beat.

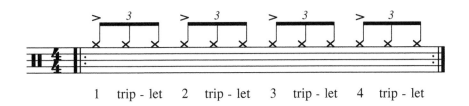

"I Just Wanna Be With You" is a shuffle blues. *Shuffle blues* is a dance-oriented, big-band style from the 1930s. To hear more shuffle blues, listen to artists such as Count Basie, Benny Goodman, the Squirrel Nut Zippers, Ray Charles, Diane Schuur, Charlie Parker, Louis Jordan, Cherry Poppin' Daddies, and Big Bad Voodoo Daddy.

LESSON 9
TECHNIQUE/THEORY

LISTEN 11 PLAY

Listen to "I Just Wanna Be With You," and then play along with the recording. Try to match the drums.

LEARNING THE BEAT

To learn the beat, follow these three steps:

1. Start with the hi-hat.
2. Add the snare drum.
3. Add the bass drum.

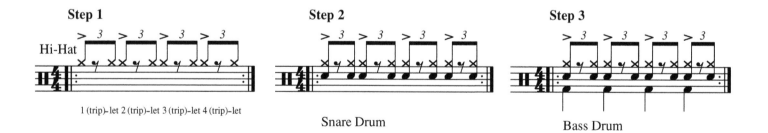

LESSON 10
LEARNING THE GROOVE

SWING

LISTEN **11** PLAY

Listen to "I Just Wanna Be With You" and focus on the cymbals. This tune is a shuffle, like "Do It Now." There is a triplet feel under each beat. The main difference is that in this tune, the middle triplet of each beat is left out. This is common in swing.

12/8 Shuffle
("Do It Now")

Double Shuffle
("I Just Wanna Be With You")

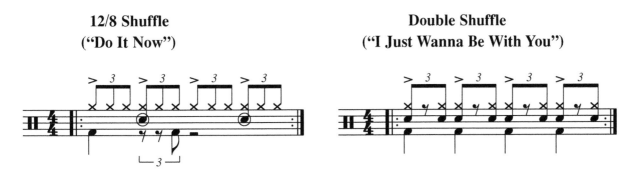

This syncopated "push-pull" feel is basic to jazz and r&b. Sometimes, this feel is called a "double shuffle" because the drummer plays the same rhythm with both hands. In this shuffle, the bass plays a "walking" quarter-note bass line.

SWING EIGHTH NOTES

Eighth notes in shuffle grooves are usually played as triplets, even though they may be notated as *straight* eighth notes.

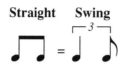

Though these rhythms look different, in some styles, they are played the same. For example, you might see the written part below on a notated jazz, shuffle, or blues chart.

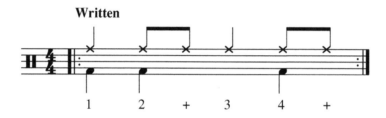

This is simpler to read than the same part, notated using triplets. Interpreting straight eighth-note rhythms as triplets is called "swinging the eighth notes."

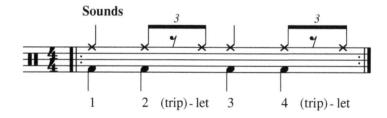

Sometimes, the word "swing," "swing feel," or "shuffle" appears on the lead sheet, telling you how to play the eighth notes. Often, though, you will just try it both ways and choose which fits the groove best. The style of the tune may help you choose whether to swing your eighth notes or play them straight.

HOOKING UP TO SWING

Practice this beat along with the recording. Play the hi-hat with your right hand. Count the triplets out loud.

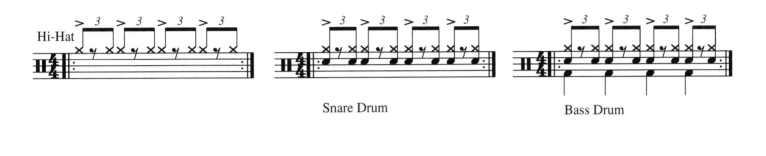

Snare Drum

Bass Drum

PRACTICE TIPS

1. Keep this feel loose and relaxed.
2. Pay attention to the balance between the snare drum and the cymbals. The snare should be slightly softer, with a small accent on beats 2 and 4.

VARIATIONS

Practice these other shuffle beats along with the recording.

1. Simplified Shuffle

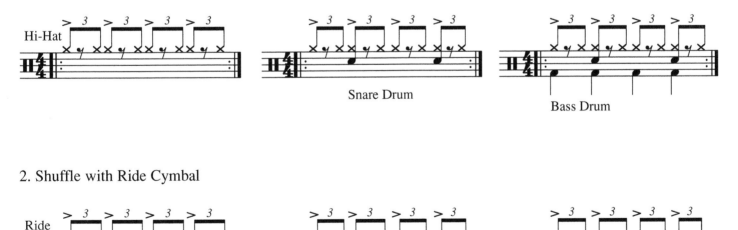

Snare Drum

Bass Drum

2. Shuffle with Ride Cymbal

Ride

Snare Drum

Bass Drum
Hi-Hat Foot

LESSON 11
IMPROVISATION

FORM AND ARRANGEMENT

"I Just Wanna Be With You" is a 12-bar blues tune. The form of each chorus is twelve measures long and divided into three phrases, just like "Do It Now." Listen for when the chords change.

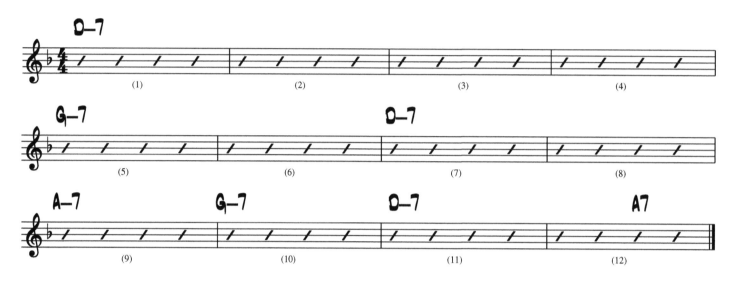

SING THE BASS

LISTEN **11** PLAY

Listen again, follow the chord chart, and sing the bass note on the downbeat of each measure.

ARRANGEMENT

LISTEN **11** PLAY

Listen to "I Just Wanna Be With You." Is there an introduction or ending? What part of the form did these added sections come from? This is the arrangement used on the recording:

INTRO	HEAD: 2x	SAX SOLO: 2x	HEAD	ENDING
4 MEASURES	‖: 1 CHORUS = 12 MEASURES :‖	‖: 1 CHORUS = 12 MEASURES :‖	1 CHORUS = 12 MEASURES ‖	8 MEASURES ‖

The intro and ending come from the form's last four measures. On the recording, the band chose to play the ending twice. This kind of repeated ending is called a *tag ending*.

CALL AND RESPONSE

1. Echo each beat, exactly as you hear it.
2. Improvise an answer to each beat. Imitate its sound and rhythmic feel.

READING

DRUM PART

LISTEN **12** PLAY

Play "I Just Wanna Be With You" while reading from the written drum part. Play it as written. Be sure to play the eighth notes with triplet "swing" feel.

I JUST WANNA BE WITH YOU

DRUM PART

BY MATT MARVUGLIO

LEAD SHEET

Now play "I Just Wanna Be With You" from the lead sheet, using your own beats and fills. There are two new notation items here:

$(\! \, \overset{>}{\! \! \! \! } \,)$ Break your regular beat when you see this (last measure) and play this rhythm instead.

INTRO/ENDING   Though this lead sheet doesn't show an introduction or ending, you and your band can create your own. The intro can be just drums, as you saw in "Do It Now," or it can come from the last line of the tune, as it does in the recording of this tune. Tag the ending at least three times, repeating the last four measures of the written part.

I JUST WANNA BE WITH YOU

BY MATT MARVUGLIO

Create your own beat and fills to "I Just Wanna Be With You." Practice it with the recording, and memorize it.

SUMMARY

FORM
12-BAR BLUES
(1 CHORUS = 12 BARS)

ARRANGEMENT
INTRO: 4 M.
2 CHORUS MELODY
2 CHORUS SOLO
1 CHORUS MELODY
END: 6 M.

SWING BEAT

PLAY "I JUST WANNA BE WITH YOU" WITH YOUR OWN BAND!

CHAPTER III
DAILY PRACTICE ROUTINE

STICK CONTROL PRACTICE

These exercises will help you play 12/8, swing, and shuffle feels. Use a metronome, and start each exercise slowly, gradually increasing your speed. Repeat each line at least ten times before continuing to the next one.

1. Stick Control

RLLRLLRLLRLL   RLLRLLRLLRLR   LRRLRRLRRLRR   LRRLRRLRRLRL

2. Double Paradiddle

RLRLRRLRLRLL

3. Inverted Double Paradiddle

RLLRLRLRRLRL   RLLRLLRLLRLR   LRRLRLRLLRLR   LRRLRRLRRLRL

4. Stick Control

RLRLRLRLRLRL   RRLLRRLLRRLL

5. a. Parradiddle-diddle

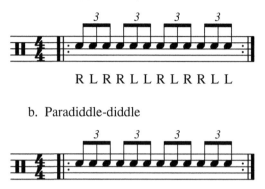

R L R R L L R L R R L L

b. Paradiddle-diddle

R L R R L L R L R R L L

6. Reading Triplets. Count the triplets aloud.

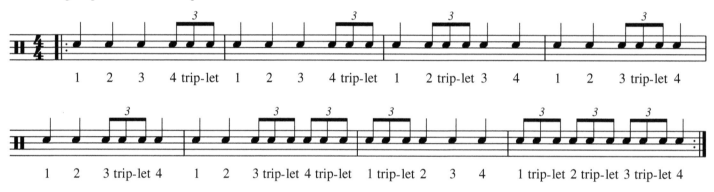

1   2   3   4 trip-let   1   2   3   4 trip-let   1   2 trip-let 3   4   1   2   3 trip-let 4

1   2   3 trip-let 4   1   2   3 trip-let 4 trip-let   1 trip-let 2   3   4   1 trip-let 2 trip-let 3 trip-let 4

"Leave Me Alone" is a *funk* tune. Funk has its roots in New Orleans street music. It started in the 1960s and is a combination of rock, r&b, Motown, jazz, and blues. Funk has also influenced many rap artists. To hear more funk, listen to artists such as James Brown, Tower of Power, Kool and the Gang, the Yellowjackets, Chaka Khan, the Meters, and Tina Turner.

LESSON 13
TECHNIQUE/THEORY

LISTEN **15** PLAY

Listen to "Leave Me Alone," and then play along with the recording. Try to match the drum part. In this tune, you will play this beat.

LEARNING THE BEAT

To learn the beat, follow these three steps:

      1. Start with the hi-hat.
      2. Add the snare drum.
      3. Add the bass drum.

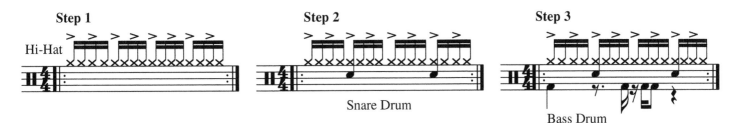

SNARE HAND: RIMSHOTS

The drummer on the recording plays rimshots on the backbeat. When you play a rimshot, you hit the snare's rim and head at exactly the same time. Can you do it softly? It takes a lot of control.

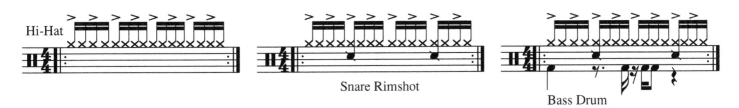

RIDE HAND: SIXTEENTH NOTES

The ride hand plays steady sixteenth notes:

    1 e + a 2 e + a 3 e + a 4 e + a

To play these up-tempo, try accenting every other note. This emphasizes the eighth note:

    >   >   >   >   >   >   >   >
    1 e + a 2 e + a 3 e + a 4 e + a
    1   +   2   +   3   +   4   +

When you accent the sixteenth notes properly, you will feel the stick bounce in your hand. This natural, bouncy stick motion gives the groove a slight swing feel (or *lilt*).

ALTERNATE STICKING

You can make this groove easier to play by using *alternate sticking*, switching hands on every sixteenth note. You will lose the hi-hat on the first sixteenth note of beats 2 and 4, but it is easier to play.

Practice this beat using alternate sticking. While it is easier for your hands, there are places where your snare hand must play simultaneously with the bass drum. Make sure that doesn't influence your hi-hat's volume or rhythm. When you feel comfortable, play this beat along with the recording.

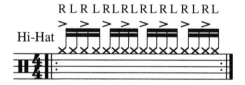

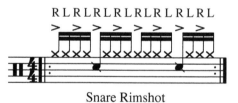

Snare Rimshot

Bass Drum

THE EASIEST BEAT THAT WILL WORK

This beat will work well for "Leave Me Alone." Play eighth notes with one hand. A variation to try, especially between bars 9 and 10, is adding another bass drum eighth note on the "+" of beat 4. This gives the section a little lift, and prepares it for the next chorus. As the song progresses, this extra bass drum note is added more often. When you feel comfortable, play this beat along with the recording.

RUFFS

A *ruff* is one of the thirteen basic rudiments. It is a full stroke preceded by two softer grace notes. Ruffs are often used for fills and setups, in all styles of music. There is a nice example of a *ruff* going into bar 4 of this tune. Listen for it in the snare drum. Can you hear the two grace notes?

Practice ruffs. The Daily Practice Routine at the end of this chapter has more ruff exercises.

LESSON 14
LEARNING THE GROOVE

FUNK

 LISTEN **15** PLAY

Listen to "Leave Me Alone." This funk groove has its roots in New Orleans street music—funky march music played on marching instruments (snare drums, bass drums, and so on) still found in the Mardi Gras parades each spring. Many New Orleans artists were important to the development of funk.

Funk rhythms are played with less of a swing feel than blues. There is an underlying sixteenth-note feel, similar to rock. Beats 2 and 4 are often accented, usually by the snare drum.

HOOKING UP

Listen to how the bass is locked in with the bass drum. The only time the bass drum plays on a downbeat is on beat 1. For the remainder of the beats, the bass drum and bass guitar play a game of "cat and mouse" with the downbeats, playing in between the cracks. Nearly every bass note hooks up with the bass drum. This adds to the "funkiness" of the groove.

During the melody, the keyboard and guitar hook up with the snare drum, playing their chords on the backbeat. For the solo choruses, their parts change to a Bo Diddley type of part (as in the song, "Who Do You Love?"), starting on the downbeat of each bar.

LESSON 15
IMPROVISATION

FORM

This funk tune follows the 12-bar blues form.

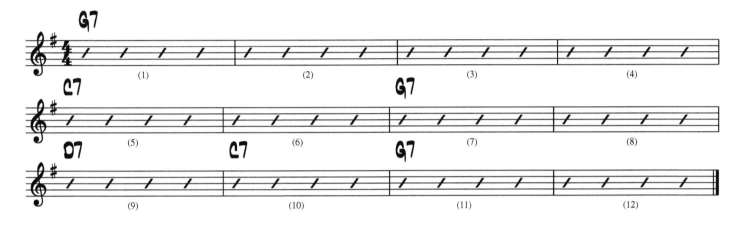

SING THE BASS

LISTEN **15** PLAY

Listen again, follow the chord chart, and sing the bass note on the downbeat of each measure.

ARRANGEMENT

On the recording, the arrangement begins with a four-measure introduction, featuring the rhythm section playing the groove.

INTRO	HEAD: 2x	SOLO: 2x	HEAD
4 MEASURES	1 CHORUS = 12 BARS	1 CHORUS = 12 BARS	1 CHORUS = 12 BARS

IDEAS FOR IMPROVISING

Fills

At the end of each chorus, the drummer plays a fill. This helps connect the sections and gives the tune a sense of shape. It is the drummer's job to "drive the bus" here, and set the general energy level for the chorus that follows. These fills are sometimes three beats long. Though they are improvised, they keep the sixteenth-note feel all the way through, and never go out of time.

Use your ear, and copy the fill at the end of the first solo chorus. Where does the drummer go from here? Hi-hat? Ride?

Practice improvising fills with a sixteenth-note feel. It is common to embellish the hi-hat. Things get nice and loose in the solos, when the ride cymbal starts. The feeling is more spacious, there are more embellishments, more colors, and more improvisations.

Listen for the cymbal crashes in the last chorus. They help keep the energy high. Can you find them?

CALL AND RESPONSE

1. Echo each beat, exactly as you hear it.
2. Improvise an answer to each beat. Imitate the sound and rhythmic feel.

LESSON 16
READING

DRUM PART

Play "Leave Me Alone" along with the recording, using the written drum part.

LEAVE ME ALONE
DRUM PART

BY MATT MARVUGLIO

LEAD SHEET

LISTEN 16 PLAY

Play "Leave Me Alone" along with the recording, and follow the lead sheet. Create your own part.

LEAVE ME ALONE

BY MATT MARVUGLIO

"FUNKY" ♩ = 82

MEMORIZE

LISTEN **16** PLAY

Create your own beat and fills to "Leave Me Alone." Practice your part with the recording, and memorize it.

SUMMARY

FORM
12-BAR BLUES
(1 CHORUS = 12 BARS)

ARRANGEMENT
INTRO: 4 M.
2 CHORUS MELODY
2 CHORUS SOLO
1 CHORUS MELODY

FUNK BEAT

PLAY "LEAVE ME ALONE" WITH YOUR OWN BAND!

CHAPTER IV
DAILY PRACTICE ROUTINE

RUFF PRACTICE

Here are three ways to play ruffs. The first one is the most common, but you should practice all three.

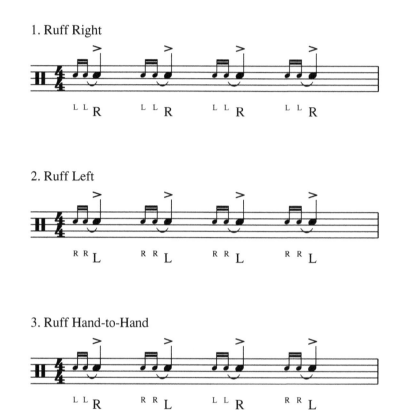

1. Ruff Right

L L R   L L R   L L R   L L R

2. Ruff Left

R R L   R R L   R R L   R R L

3. Ruff Hand-to-Hand

L L R   R R L   L L R   R R L

STICKING CONTROL EXERCISE

This sticking control exercise will help you develop your technique for ruffs.

RLLRLLRLLRLL   RLLRLLRLLRLR   LRRLRRLRRLRR   LRRLRRLRRLRL

"Affordable" is another funk tune, but it is lighter, with more of a feeling of open space. This style is popular with smooth-jazz artists. To hear more light funk, listen to artists such as David Sanborn, Earl Klugh, Walter Beasley, the Rippingtons, Dave Grusin, Kenny G, Bob James, and Anita Baker.

LESSON 17
TECHNIQUE/THEORY

LISTEN 19 PLAY

Listen to "Affordable," and then play along with the recording. Try to match the drum part. This tune has two parts.

LEARNING THE BEAT

To learn the beat, follow these three steps:

1. Start with the hi-hat.
2. Add the snare drum (only the second beat).
3. Add the bass drum.

In the first part, the drums play this two-measure beat:

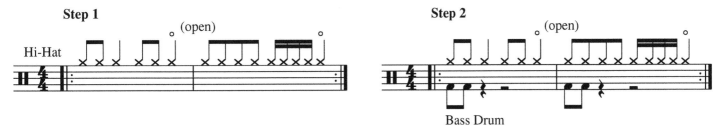

In the second part, the drums play this beat:

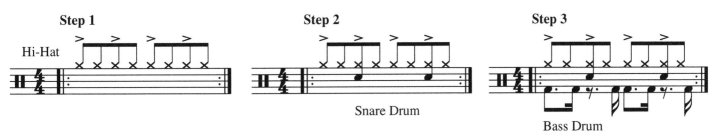

Play along with the recording and match the drums.

CHAPTER V

HI-HAT

This tune makes good use of the hi-hat. There are many sound possibilities for the hi-hat that you should keep in mind when you are playing. Experiment with some of these ways of controlling the sound.

1. Tight or loose. Try changing how much pressure you use with your foot, and open it to a variety of different widths.

2. Surface. Try hitting different surfaces of the hi-hat. There is a different sound on the edge, in the middle, and on the bell.

3. Stick. Hit the different parts of the hi-hat with different parts of the stick. Use the tip, the shoulder, and the side.

Experiment with these possibilities, and find the ones that fit the music and your personal taste.

LESSON 18
LEARNING THE GROOVE

LIGHT FUNK

Listen to "Affordable." This groove is built around eighth notes, with some syncopated sixteenths in the B section. Notice that the band hooks up with the bass drum on the dotted-eighth/sixteenth rhythm.

To learn this feel, practice counting sixteenths, leaving out the middle two sixteenths of each beat. Count out loud, along with a metronome or click track on the quarter-note pulse.

This rhythm is usually written out like this:

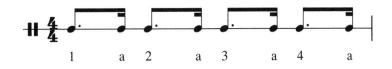

PRACTICE TIP

When you are learning a new beat, sing your part before you play it.

HOOKING UP

The melody of "Affordable" is mostly made up of long, sustained notes. Listening to the rest of the rhythm section and counting will help you keep your place.

The bass drum and bass guitar play identical rhythms throughout the tune. Take care to play in synch at all times. Notice how the hi-hat is used to fill spaces and how fills are used to set up transitions to different sections.

LESSON 19
IMPROVISATION

FORM AND ARRANGEMENT

LISTEN **19** PLAY

Listen to "Affordable" and follow the saxophone melody over the 16-bar form.

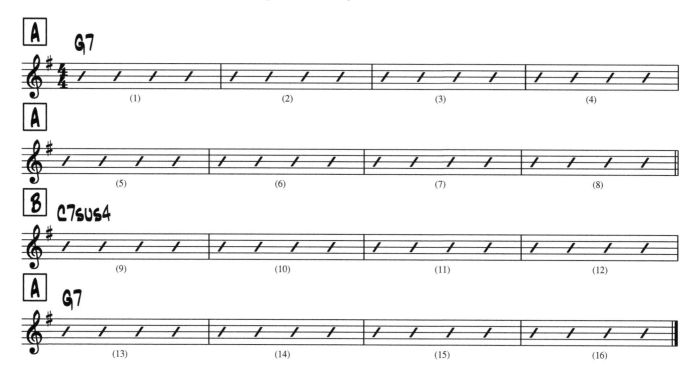

As you have already seen from practicing the beats, there are two primary musical ideas in this tune. The sax plays contrasting melodies over them. Idea A is very sparse. It lasts for eight measures, with two phrases of sax melody. Idea B is in a more regular rhythm. It lasts for four measures. Then Idea A returns for four measures. This form can be described simply as "AABA."

> **PRACTICE TIP**
>
> Imagine the melody as you play your beats. This will help you keep your place—particularly during improvised solos, when nobody plays the melody. Although the form of this tune is simple, it is easy to get lost. The 4-measure return of Idea A at the end of the form may be confused with the eight measures of Idea A that begin the new chorus. Altogether, there are twelve measures of this idea, so keep careful count.

SING THE BASS

LISTEN **19** PLAY

Listen again, follow the chord chart, and sing the bass note on the downbeat of each measure.

VARIATIONS

LISTEN **20** PLAY

Here's another beat you can use for the second part of this tune. When you can play it comfortably, practice it along with the recording.

Sixteenth-Note Feel

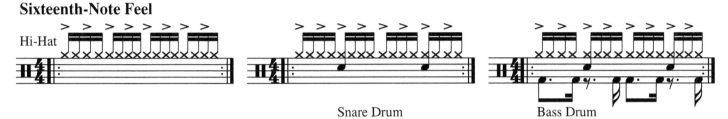

Snare Drum   Bass Drum

CALL AND RESPONSE

1. Echo each beat, exactly as you hear it.
2. Improvise an answer to each beat. Imitate its sound and rhythmic feel.

LISTEN **21** PLAY

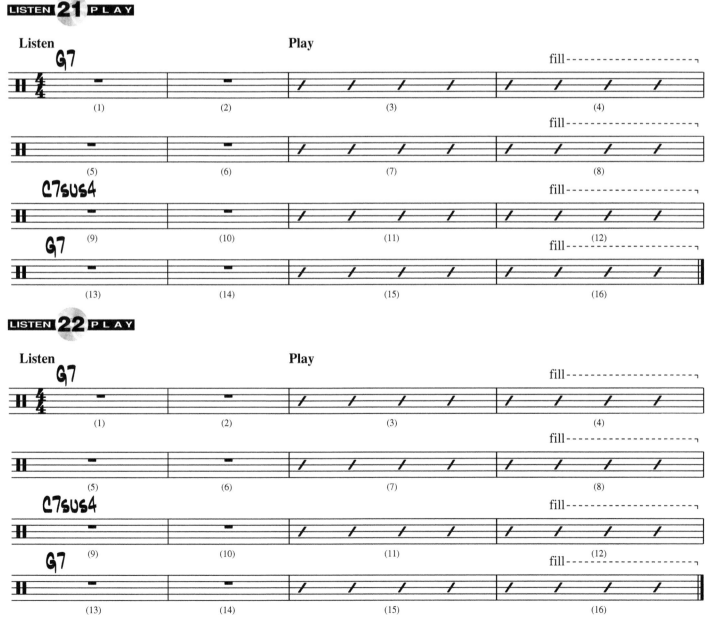

LESSON 20
READING

DRUM PART

LISTEN **20** PLAY

Play "Affordable" along with the recording. Use the written drum part.

$\frac{2}{\text{//}}$ Two-measure repeat. Repeat the previously-notated two measures.

AFFORDABLE

"LIGHT FUNK" ♩ = 84

DRUM PART

BY MATT MARVUGLIO

54

LEAD SHEET

LISTEN **20** PLAY

Play "Affordable" along with the recording, and follow the lead sheet. Create your own part.

AFFORDABLE

By Matt Marvuglio

"Light Funk" ♩ = 84

MEMORIZE

LISTEN **20** PLAY

Create your own beat and fills to "Affordable." Practice along with the recording, and memorize your part.

SUMMARY

FORM	ARRANGEMENT	LIGHT FUNK BEAT
16-Bar AABA	Intro: 8 M.	
(1 chorus = 16 bars)	1 Chorus Melody	
A: 4 M.	1 Chorus Solo	
B: 4 M.	1 Chorus Melody	

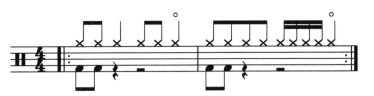

PLAY "AFFORDABLE" WITH YOUR OWN BAND!

CHAPTER V
DAILY PRACTICE ROUTINE

STICK CONTROL EXERCISES

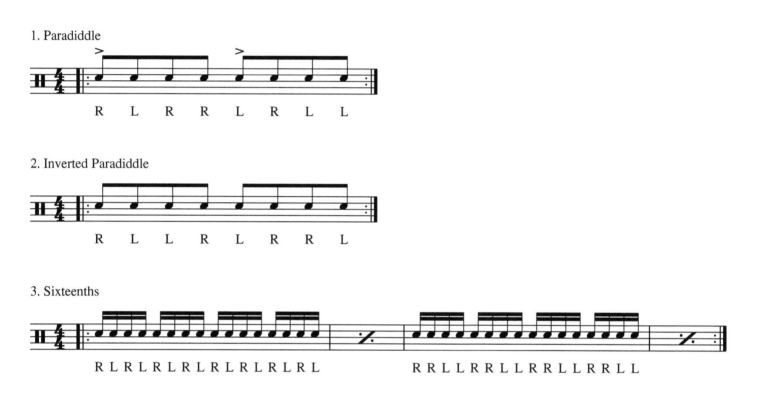

1. Paradiddle

R L R R L R L L

2. Inverted Paradiddle

R L L R L R R L

3. Sixteenths

R L R L R L R L R L R L R L R L   R R L L R R L L R R L L R R L L

READING EXERCISE

Practice this exercise, and focus on keeping the volume even between your hands. Notice that the rhythms in measures 2 and 4 sound the same, though they are notated differently. The way it appears in measure 4 is the more common way of writing it.

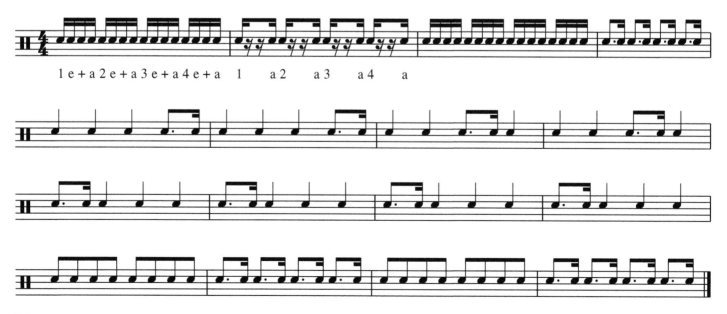

1 e + a 2 e + a 3 e + a 4 e + a   1   a 2   a 3   a 4   a

"Don't Look Down" is a *hard rock* tune. Hard rock first appeared in the late 1960s. It has characteristic heavy bass, long, drawn-out chords, and amplified instruments. To hear more hard rock, listen to artists such as Aerosmith, Metallica, Powerman 5000, the Allman Brothers Band, Rob Zombie, Godsmack, 311, Stone Temple Pilots, Black Crowes, Steve Vai, and Smashing Pumpkins.

LESSON 21
TECHNIQUE/THEORY

LISTEN **23** PLAY

Listen to "Don't Look Down," and then play along with the recording. Try to match the drum part. This tune has two parts.

LEARNING THE BEAT

To learn the beat, follow these three steps:

      1. Start with the hi-hat.
      2. Add the snare drum.
      3. Add the bass drum.

This is the beat to the first part:

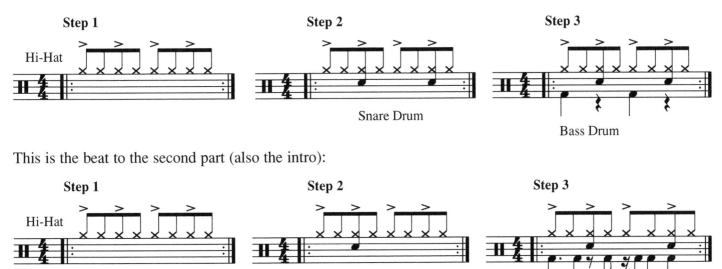

This is the beat to the second part (also the intro):

Play "Don't Look Down" along with the recording. Hook up with the groove.

RIDE HAND

Listen to the continuous eighth notes. Each downbeat (eighth note *on* the beat) uses a downstroke, and each upbeat (eighth note *off* the beat) uses an upstroke. Practice playing the bass drum without affecting the feel of the ride hand, especially in the second beat.

Keep the hi-hat closed during the first part. During the second part, play it with the foot on beats 2 and 4.

> **PRACTICE TIP**
>
> Vary your intensity on the hi-hat notes. Develop your sense of where on the surface to play, and how open to keep the cymbals. This will help you create different levels of "wash."

SNARE HAND

Play a solid snare backbeat.

FOOT

The bass drum part in the second beat is syncopated, which makes it tricky. Keep your foot independent of your hands, so that your eighth notes don't get louder when they coincide with the bass drum.

FLAMS

A *flam* is a normal stroke closely preceded by a softer stroke (grace note). One reason that the ending of "Don't Look Down" sounds so powerful is that the drummer is playing flams. Flams are two attacks played so closely together that they sound like one big attack.

Practice flams, alternating hands.

LESSON 22
LEARNING THE GROOVE

HARD ROCK

LISTEN 23 PLAY

Listen to "Don't Look Down." This tune has a standard rock/metal groove. It is a heavy feel, with very simple drum and bass parts. These parts must be simple because they are intended to be played in large arenas, where echoes would make busier parts sound muddy. It's a case of "less is more."

Eighth notes are played straight, not with a swing feel. The bass drum plays on beats 1 and 3, which is typical of rock drum beats.

HOOKING UP WITH THE BAND

This tune has an active bass part and a relatively straight-ahead drum part, which is different than the other tunes we've been playing. On the second part, the guitar and bass play the riff *in unison* (together). This is a big, powerful sound. The keyboard plays long, sustained chords. The drums are the glue, keeping the strong backbeat on the snare, and crashing on each bar's downbeat.

LESSON 23
IMPROVISATION

FORM AND ARRANGEMENT

LISTEN **23** PLAY

Listen to the recording and try to figure out the form and arrangement by ear. How long does each section of the form last? Is there an introduction or ending? For how many measures or beats does each chord last? Write down as much information as you can. Check your answers against the summary later in this chapter.

This tune has a 20-bar AB form. Part A has an active riff that builds a lot of tension. It lasts for sixteen measures. Part B is less active than the first part. It lasts for four measures. There is a 4-measure introduction at the beginning of the tune that comes from the B section.

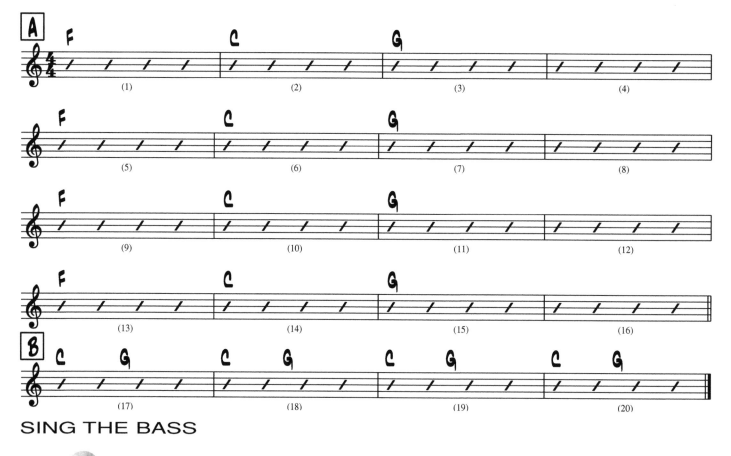

SING THE BASS

LISTEN **23** PLAY

Listen again, follow the chord chart, and sing the bass note on the downbeat of each measure.

> **PERFORMANCE TIP**
>
> On the recording, when the power melody returns at the coda, the drum plays on the toms. This helps create a big sound on the ending.

CALL AND RESPONSE

1. Echo each beat, exactly as you hear it.
2. Improvise an answer to each beat. Imitate its sound and rhythmic feel.

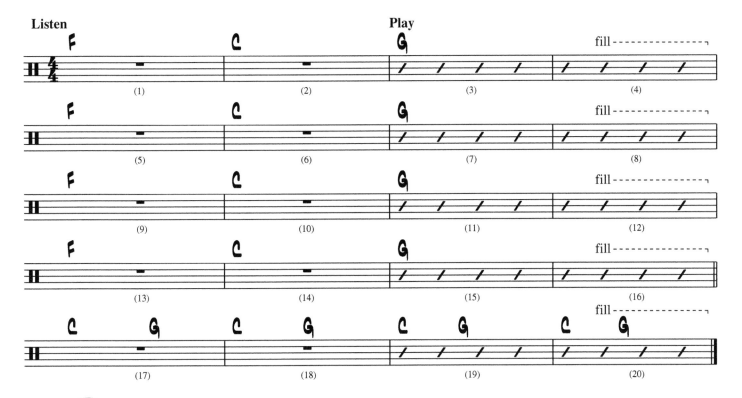

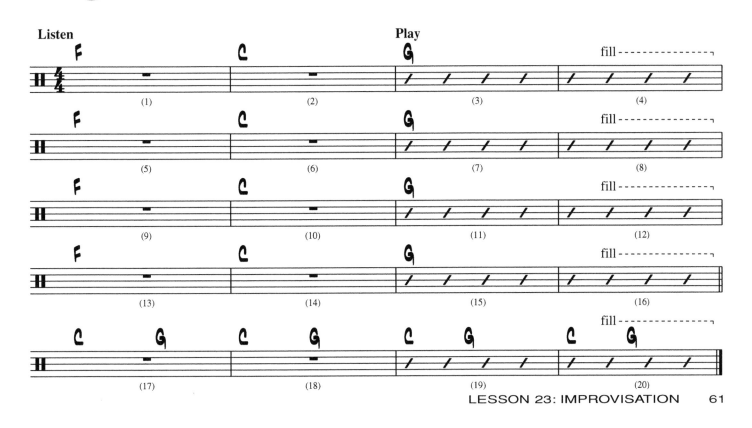

DRUM PART

|1. |2.

:||

First and second ending markings. The first time you play these measures, play the *first ending*—the measures under the number 1.

Then return to the begin-repeat sign (||:). The second time, skip the first ending and play the *second ending*—the measures under the number 2. Then, continue through the rest of the form.

Play "Don't Look Down" along with the recording. Use the written drum part.

DON'T LOOK DOWN
DRUM PART
BY MATT MARVUGLIO

LEAD SHEET

Play your own part to "Don't Look Down" and follow the lead sheet.

MEMORIZE

Create your own beat and fills to "Don't Look Down." Practice it along with the recording, and memorize your part.

SUMMARY

FORM
20-BAR AB FORM
(1 CHORUS = 20 BARS)
A: 16 M.
B: 4 M.

ARRANGEMENT
INTRO: 4 M.
1 CHORUS MELODY
1 CHORUS SOLO
1 CHORUS MELODY
END: 2 M.

HARD ROCK BEATS

PLAY "DON'T LOOK DOWN" WITH YOUR OWN BAND!

CHAPTER VI
DAILY PRACTICE ROUTINE

FLAM PRACTICE

These exercises will help you develop your flam technique.

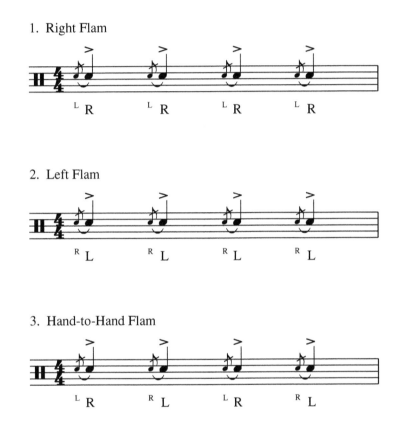

1. Right Flam

2. Left Flam

3. Hand-to-Hand Flam

"Take Your Time" is a *bossa nova* tune. Bossa nova began in Brazil, combining American jazz and an Afro-Brazilian form of dance music called *samba*. To hear more bossa nova, listen to Stan Getz, Antonio Carlos Jobim, Eliane Elias, Astrud Gilberto, Flora Purim, Dave Valentine, and João Gilberto.

LESSON 25
TECHNIQUE/THEORY

LISTEN **27** PLAY

Listen to "Take Your Time" and then play along with the recording. Try to match the drum part. On this beat, first get the feel of the hi-hat and bass drum, and then add the snare drum.

LEARNING THE BEAT

To learn the beat, follow these four steps:

1. Start with the hi-hat.
2. Add the bass drum.
3. Add the first measure of the snare drum.
4. Add the second measure of the snare drum.

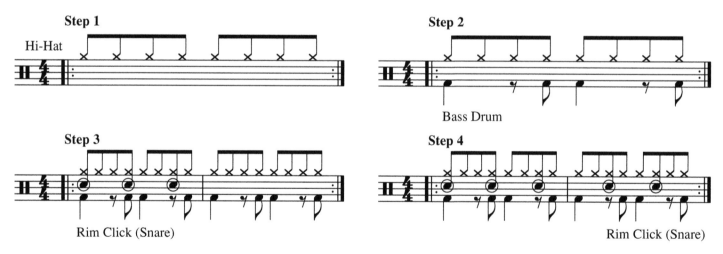

BOSSA NOVA TECHNIQUE

In bossa nova, the rim click and bass drum should be softer than what you would play in rock or blues. Play with a smooth, relaxed feel, and light dynamics. Try orchestrating the rhythms using different sounds, such as the tom-toms.

PRACTICE TIP

Practice slowly at first to gain control over your coordination. Internalize the feeling of the two-bar syncopated phrase. Listen to recordings of other bossa nova tunes, and try to imitate them, when you play.

LESSON 26
LEARNING THE GROOVE

BOSSA NOVA

LISTEN **27** PLAY

Listen to "Take Your Time." This tune is a bossa nova, a style of music that originated in Brazil. Throughout the tune, a two-bar rhythmic pattern repeats. This repeating pattern is an essential part of bossa nova. The drummer plays it as a rim click.

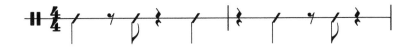

Repeating rhythmic structures are at the heart of much African-based music, including Afro-Caribbean and most South and Latin American styles.

HOOKING UP

Count steady eighth notes while you clap the two-bar rhythm. First practice this by yourself, and then try it along with the recording.

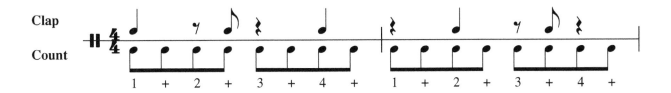

LESSON 27
IMPROVISATION

FORM

Listen to "Take Your Time" and follow the form. This tune follows a 16-bar AB form. Each phrase of the melody lasts for eight measures.

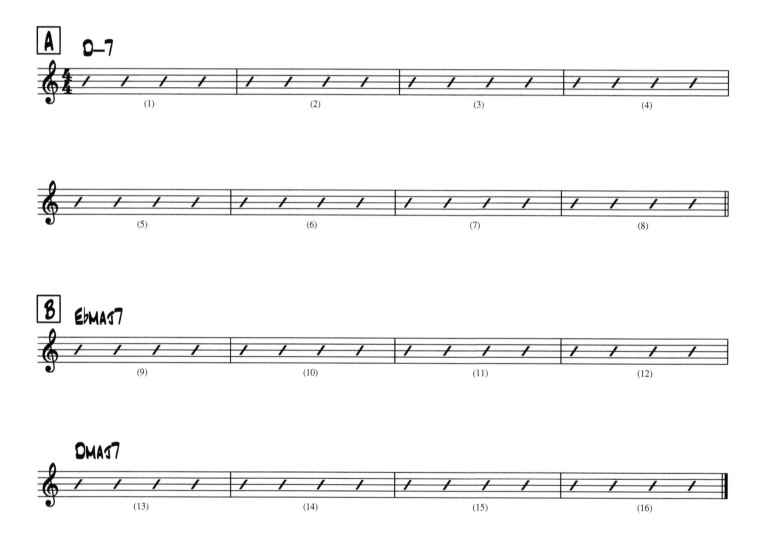

SING THE BASS

Listen again, follow the chord chart, and sing the bass note on the downbeat of each measure.

ARRANGEMENT

What is the arrangement on the recording? Figure it out by ear, and then check your answer against the summary later in this chapter.

VARIATIONS

LISTEN **28** PLAY

Practice these beats. When you are comfortable with them, practice them along with the recording.

Variation 1

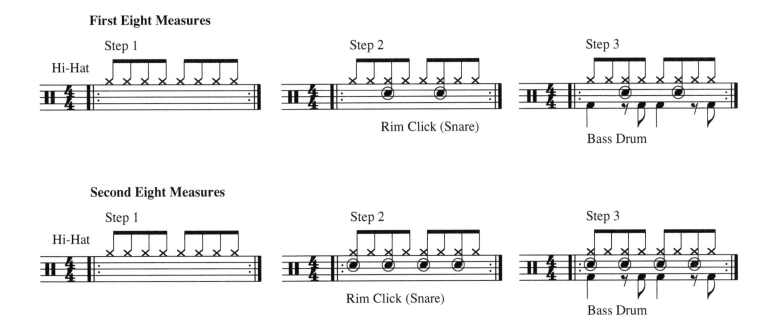

Variation 2

In this variation, you will use the ride cymbal instead of the hi-hat for the first eight measures.

First Eight Measures

Step 1
Ride

Step 2
Bass Drum   Hi-Hat Foot

Step 3
Snare Drum

Step 4
Snare Drum

Second Eight Measures

Step 1
Hi-Hat

Step 2
Bass Drum

Step 3
Snare Drum

Step 4
Snare Drum

CALL AND RESPONSE

1. Echo each beat, exactly as you hear it.
2. Improvise an answer to each beat. Imitate its sound and rhythmic feel.

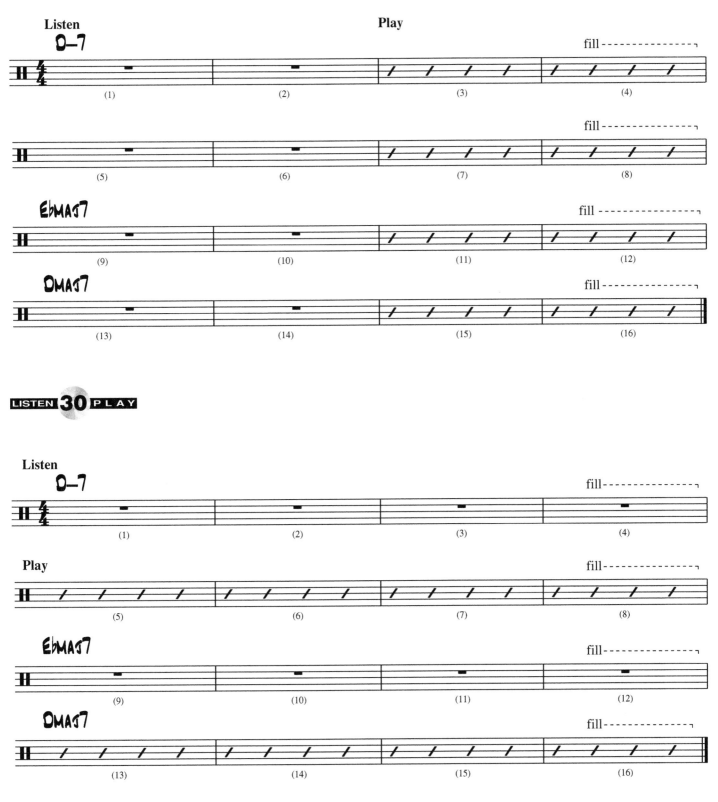

LESSON 28
READING

DRUM PART

Play "Take Your Time" and use the written drum part.

LISTEN 28 PLAY

TAKE YOUR TIME
DRUM PART
By Matt Marvuglio

LEAD SHEET

LISTEN **28** PLAY

Play "Take Your Time" and follow the lead sheet. Create your own bossa nova beats and practice them with the recording.

MEMORIZE

LISTEN **28** PLAY

Create your own bossa nova beats and fills to "Take Your Time." Practice along with the recording, and memorize your part.

SUMMARY

FORM
16-BAR AB
(1 CHORUS = 16 BARS)
A: 8 M.
B: 8 M.

ARRANGEMENT
INTRO: 8 M.
2 CHORUS MELODY
2 CHORUS SOLO
1 CHORUS MELODY
END: 8 M.

BOSSA NOVA BEAT

PLAY "TAKE YOUR TIME" WITH YOUR OWN BAND!

CHAPTER VII
DAILY PRACTICE ROUTINE

STICK CONTROL EXERCISES

When you practice these exercises, strive for an even sound between your hands.

1. Stick Control 1

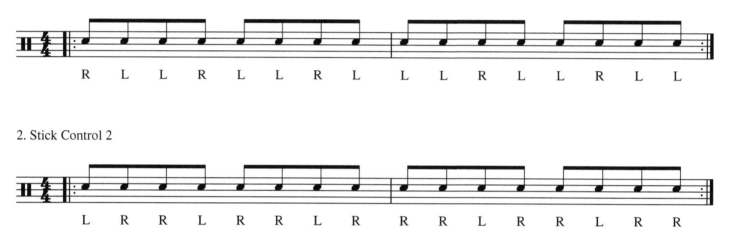

2. Stick Control 2

FLAMS

Practice these flam patterns, and use them in your bossa nova beats.

1. Flam Bossa 1

2. Flam Bossa 2

"Stop It" is a blues/jazz tune in which *stop time* accents the melody, like a question and answer. Stop time is very common in blues, jazz, and other styles. To hear more stop time blues, listen to artists such as Miles Davis, John Coltrane, Jim Hall, Sarah Vaughn, Bill Evans, Ella Fitzgerald, Louis Armstrong, Abbie Lincoln, Dizzy Gillespie, and Charlie Parker.

LESSON 29
TECHNIQUE/THEORY

LISTEN 31 PLAY

Listen to "Stop It" and then play along with the recording.

LEARNING THE BEAT

To learn the beat, follow these three steps:
1. Start with the hi-hat or ride.
2. Add the snare drum and tom-tom (only the first beat).
3. Add the bass drum.

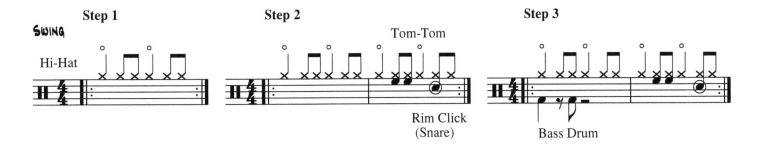

During the solos, the drums play this beat:

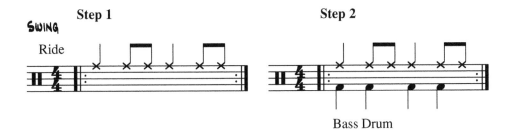

CHAPTER VIII

HI-HAT

This groove has a repeating two-measure jazz-swing beat. Keep the hi-hat closed to get a tight, dry sound. Open it slightly on the note leading to beat 3, first measure only. Close it again for beat 4, and through the second measure.

BASS DRUM

During solos, the drums play a steady beat. The bass guitar plays a walking line—steady quarter notes. You can help reinforce the bass's walk with a very soft bass drum on every beat. This is called *feathering* the bass drum—so light that you could be playing it with a feather. It should be felt more than heard.

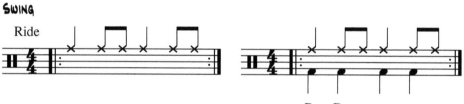

LESSON 30
LEARNING THE GROOVE

STOP-TIME BLUES

LISTEN **31** P L A Y

Listen to "Stop It." This jazz cymbal beat is at the heart of jazz rhythm. The "spang spang a-lang" cymbal beat is unique to jazz, and it has been its primary pattern since the 1940s. Its underlying pulse is the same as the shuffle. This pattern has accompanied Louis Armstrong, Count Basie, Miles Davis, John Coltrane, Duke Ellington, and thousands of other jazz artists.

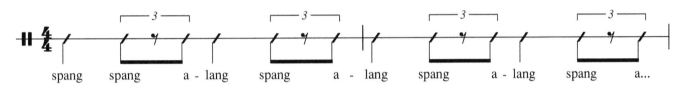

In stop time, the groove is punctuated by *stop-time kicks*. These are rhythmic figures, usually just one or two beats long, that punctuate the melody. That is why it is called "stop time"—the melody "stops" or rests. It is very important that you keep an accurate pulse through these areas where you do not play. Since the accented eighth note is an anticipated third beat, it makes sense to start counting on 4.

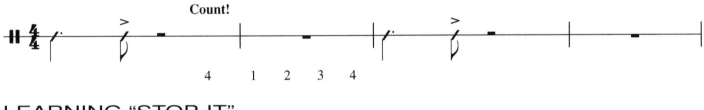

LEARNING "STOP IT"

At the head, the drums plays both parts—the stop time kicks on the bass drum and the jazz cymbal beat on the hi-hat (it moves to the ride during solos). The hi-hat opens up for the stop-time kicks, hooking up with the bass drum and the rest of the rhythm section. Practice this beat. When you can play it comfortably, practice it along with the stop-time section of "Stop It."

LISTEN **32** P L A Y

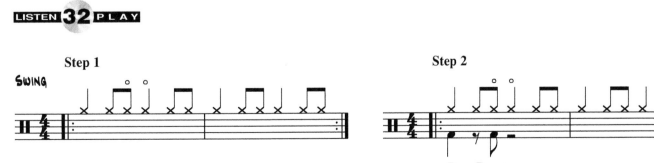

HOOKING UP

Keep the ride cymbal beat constant—the band needs it to hold together. Even just playing steady quarter notes in the cymbal will help. You can also add a "chick" to the backbeat with the hi-hat foot. Try this progression. When you can play it comfortably, practice it along with the recording.

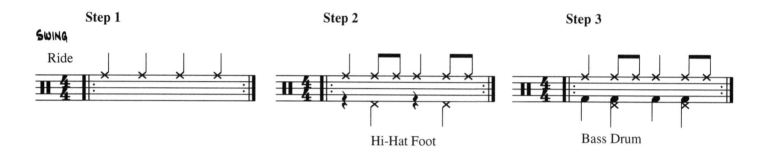

PRACTICE TIP

When you play the jazz beat on the cymbal, imagine you are playing with a paddle ball—the kind with a rubber band linking a rubber ball to a wooden paddle. Each strike of the ball is even, with forward motion. Each bounce pushes ahead, and all beats are close in intensity. This is the feeling of the ride cymbal.

On the solo section, the drums and bass hook up to provide a constant quarter-note groove over which the soloist can improvise. The guitar and keyboard play syncopated comping parts, giving the groove more motion. Here is the beat again. Remember to feather the bass drum—it should be felt more than heard.

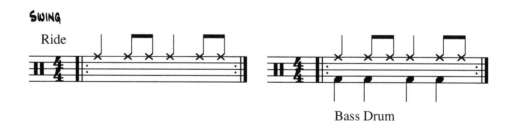

LESSON 31
IMPROVISATION

FORM AND ARRANGEMENT

LISTEN **31** PLAY

Listen to "Stop It." Try to figure out the form and arrangement by ear, and check your answer against the summary later in this chapter.

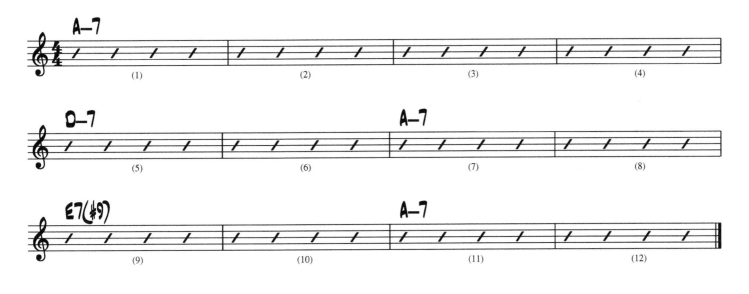

SING THE BASS

LISTEN **31** PLAY

Listen again, follow the chord chart, and sing the bass note on the downbeat of each measure.

VARIATIONS

LISTEN **34** PLAY

On the recording, the drummer varies his part. The hi-hat often opens up on beat 1, and sometimes in other places too. It always complements the soloist's part. So, in addition to doing the primary job of keeping time, the drummer should also be interacting with the other musicians, and keeping the drum part spontaneous.

Varying the snare can also make the beat more interesting. Practice each of these variations along with the recording. You can move the snare to the toms, or the hi-hat to the ride. When you can play this easily, add your own bass drum part, and then practice the beat along with the recording.

HI-HAT VARIATIONS

These variations will help you develop your hi-hat technique. Also practice them on the ride cymbal.

1. Hi-Hat Variation 1

2. Hi-Hat Variation 2

Practice the next two variations closed, at first. Then begin to open the hi-hat slightly on the upbeats (second eighth notes) of beats 2 and 4.

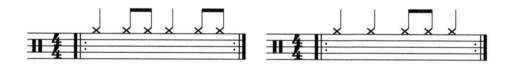

3. Hi-Hat Variation 3

CALL AND RESPONSE

1. Echo each beat, exactly as you hear it.
2. Improvise an answer to each beat. Imitate its sound and rhythmic feel.

LESSON 32
READING

DRUM PART

Play "Stop It" along with the recording and read from the written part.

D.C. AL  From the beginning, and take the coda. Jump to the very first measure of the tune, and play from there. When you reach the first coda symbol, skip ahead to the next coda symbol (at the end). This is similar to the "D.S. al Coda," but instead of going to a sign, go to the first measure of the tune.

LISTEN **34** PLAY

LEAD SHEET

LISTEN **34** PLAY

Play "Stop It" from the lead sheet. Use your own part.

STOP IT

"Swing" ♩ = 156

By Matt Marvuglio

ENDING

A–7

MEMORIZE

LISTEN **34** PLAY

Create your own beat and fills to "Stop It." Practice it with the recording, and memorize your part.

FORM
12-Bar Blues
(1 Chorus = 12 Bars)

ARRANGEMENT
2 Chorus Melody
4 Chorus Solo
2 Chorus Melody
End: 1 m.

SWING BEATS
STOP TIME

SOLOS

PLAY "STOP IT" WITH YOUR OWN BAND!

CHATER VIII
DAILY PRACTICE ROUTINE

LEFT-HAND VARIATIONS

LISTEN **34** P L A Y

Practice these variations. When you can play the complete beat comfortably, practice it along with the recording. During solos, the left hand is free to improvise figures behind the soloist. These variations will help you find some interesting things to play.

1. Variation 1

2. Variation 2

3. Variation 3

4. Variation 4

Final Remarks

Congratulations on completing the *Berklee Practice Method*. You now have a good idea of the role of the drummer in a band, and have command of the eight grooves and time feels of these tunes. The beats and fills that you have learned are important and useful parts of your musical vocabulary. In addition, you have tools and ideas for creating your own beats and fills. This is a great start!

What to do next? Play along with your favorite recordings. Find records that you hear other musicians talking about. Learn these tunes, grooves, and fills. Continue your theory, reading, and technique work. Investigate harmony. Practice reading treble and bass clef. Become a complete musician.

Develop your concept of what it means to play drums. Realize how important you are as a drummer in a band. You have a big responsibility, as the band's time keeper. It is a powerful position.

Play your drums every day, by yourself and with others, and get the rhythm in your body.

Keep the beat!

—Ron and Casey

GUITAR RECORDED VERSIONS®

AUTHENTIC TRANSCRIPTIONS WITH NOTES AND TABLATURE

Guitar Recorded Versions® are note-for-note transcriptions of guitar music taken directly off recordings. This series, one of the most popular in print today, features some of the greatest guitar players and groups from blues and rock to country and jazz.

Guitar Recorded Versions are transcribed by the best transcribers in the business. Every book contains notes and tablature unless otherwise marked. Visit **halleonard.com** for our complete selection.

Will Ackerman
00690016 The Will Ackerman Collection $24.99
Bryan Adams
00690501 Greatest Hits $24.99
Aerosmith
00690603 O Yeah! $29.99
Alice in Chains
00690178 Acoustic $22.99
00694865 Dirt $19.99
00660225 Facelift $19.99
00694925 Jar of Flies/Sap $19.99
00690387 Nothing Safe $24.99
All That Remains
00142819 The Order of Things..$22.99
Allman Brothers Band
00694932 Definitive Collection, Volume 1..................$29.99
00694933 Definitive Collection, Volume 2..................$27.99
00694934 Definitive Collection, Volume 3..................$29.99
Duane Allman
00690958 Guitar Anthology $29.99
Alter Bridge
00691071 AB III $29.99
00690945 Blackbird $24.99
00690755 One Day Remains......$24.99
Anthrax
00690849 Best of Anthrax..........$27.99
Arctic Monkeys
00123558 AM $24.99
Chet Atkins
00690158 Almost Alone $22.99
00694878 Vintage Fingerstyle.....$22.99
Audioslave
00690609 Audioslave.................$24.99
00690884 Revelations................$19.95
Avenged Sevenfold
00690926 Avenged Sevenfold $24.99
00214869 Best of: 2005-2013 ..$29.99
00690820 City of Evil $27.99
00123216 Hail to the King $27.99
00691051 Nightmare $27.99
00222486 The Stage $29.99
00691065 Waking the Fallen......$24.99
The Avett Brothers
00123140 Guitar Collection $22.99
Randy Bachman
00694918 Guitar Collection $24.99
The Beatles
00690489 1 (Number Ones) $24.99
00694929 1962-1966 ....$27.99
00694930 1967-1970 ....$29.99
00694880 Abbey Road $19.99
00694832 Acoustic Guitar..........$27.99
00691066 Beatles for Sale $22.99
00690903 Capitol Albums Vol. 2 .$24.99
00691031 Help! $19.99
00690482 Let It Be $19.99
00691030 Magical Mystery Tour..$22.99
00691067 Meet the Beatles! $22.99
00691068 Please Please Me $22.99
00694891 Revolver $22.99
00691014 Rock Band $34.99
00694914 Rubber Soul..............$24.99
00694863 Sgt. Pepper's Lonely Hearts Club Band......$22.99
00110193 Tomorrow Never Knows $22.99
00690110 White Album Book 1..$19.99
00690111 White Album Book 2..$19.99

The Beach Boys
00690503 Very Best $24.99
Beck
00690632 Beck – Sea Change ...$19.95
Jeff Beck
00691044 Best of Beck.............$24.99
00691042 Blow by Blow $22.99
00691041 Truth $19.99
00691043 Wired $19.99
George Benson
00694884 Best of......................$22.99
Chuck Berry
00692385 Chuck Berry.............$24.99
Billy Talent
00690835 Billy Talent $22.99
00690879 Billy Talent II.............$22.99
Black Crowes
00147787 Best of $24.99
The Black Keys
00129737 Turn Blue $22.99
Black Sabbath
00690149 Black Sabbath $19.99
00690901 Best of $22.99
00691010 Heaven and Hell $24.99
00690148 Master of Reality $19.99
00690142 Paranoid $19.99
00691045 Vol. 4 ....$22.99
00692200 We Sold Our Soul for Rock 'n' Roll $24.99
blink-182
00690389 Enema of the State $22.99
00690831 Greatest Hits.............$24.99
00691179 Neighborhoods..........$22.99
Michael Bloomfield
00148544 Guitar Anthology $24.99
Blue Öyster Cult
00690028 Cult Classics $22.99
Bon Jovi
00691074 Greatest Hits.............$24.99
Joe Bonamassa
00158600 Blues of Desperation $24.99
00139086 Different Shades of Blue $22.99
00198117 Muddy Wolf at Red Rocks................$24.99
00283540 Redemption $24.99
00358863 Royal Tea $24.99
Boston
00690913 Boston......................$22.99
00690829 Guitar Collection $24.99
David Bowie
00690491 Best of......................$22.99
Box Car Racer
00690583 Box Car Racer...........$19.95
Breaking Benjamin
00691023 Dear Agony $22.99
00690873 Phobia......................$22.99
Lenny Breau
00141446 Best of $19.99
Big Bill Broonzy
00286503 Guitar Collection $19.99
Roy Buchanan
00690168 Collection $24.99
Jeff Buckley
00690451 Collection.................$27.99
Bullet for My Valentine
00690957 Scream Aim Fire $22.99
00119629 Temper Temper $22.99
Kenny Burrell
00690678 Best of $24.99
Cage the Elephant
00691077 Thank You, Happy Birthday $22.99

The Cars
00691159 Complete Greatest Hits.$24.99
Carter Family
00690261 Collection.................$19.99
Johnny Cash
00691079 Best of......................$24.99
Cheap Trick
00690043 Best of......................$24.99
Chicago
00690171 Definitive Guitar Collection $29.99
Chimaira
00691011 Guitar Collection $24.99
Charlie Christian
00690567 Definitive Collection ..$22.99
Eric Church
00101916 Chief $22.99
The Civil Wars
00129545 The Civil Wars $19.99
Eric Clapton
00690590 Anthology.................$34.99
00694896 Blues Breakers (with John Mayall) $19.99
00138731 The Breeze $24.99
00691055 Clapton $22.99
00690936 Complete Clapton $34.99
00690010 From the Cradle $24.99
00192383 I Still Do $19.99
00690363 Just One Night..........$27.99
00694873 Timepieces $19.95
00694869 Unplugged................$24.99
00124873 Unplugged (Deluxe) ..$29.99
The Clash
00690162 Best of......................$22.99
Coheed & Cambria
00690828 IV $24.99
00139967 In Keeping Secrets of Silent Earth: 3 ....$24.99
Coldplay
00130786 Ghost Stories $19.99
Collective Soul
00690855 Best of $19.95
Jessee Cook
00141704 Works Vol. 1 ....$22.99
Alice Cooper
00691091 Best of......................$24.99
Counting Crows
00694940 August & Everything After.........$22.99
Robert Cray
00127184 Best of $19.99
Cream
00694840 Disraeli Gears $24.99
Creed
00288787 Greatest Hits.............$22.99
Creedence Clearwater Revival
00690819 Best of......................$27.99
Jim Croce
00690648 The Very Best $19.99
Steve Cropper
00690572 Soul Man..................$22.99
Crosby, Stills & Nash
00690613 Best of......................$29.99
Cry of Love
00691171 Brother $22.99
Dick Dale
00690637 Best of......................$22.99
Death Cab for Cutie
00690967 Narrow Stairs $22.99
Deep Purple
00690289 Best of......................$22.99
00690288 Machine Head $19.99

Def Leppard
00690784 Best of......................$24.99
Derek and the Dominos
00694831 Layla & Other Assorted Love Songs..$24.99
Ani DiFranco
00690384 Best of......................$19.95
Dinosaur Jr.
00690979 Best of $22.99
The Doors
00690347 Anthology.................$22.95
00690348 Essential Collection ...$16.95
Dream Theater
00160579 The Astonishing $24.99
00122443 Dream Theater $29.99
00291164 Distance Over Time ..$24.99
Eagles
00278631 Their Greatest Hits 1971-1975.........$22.99
00278632 Very Best of..............$39.99
Duane Eddy
00690250 Best of......................$24.99
Tommy Emmanuel
00147067 All I Want for Christmas..................$19.99
00690909 Best of $27.99
00172824 It's Never Too Late $22.99
00139220 Little by Little $24.99
Melissa Etheridge
00690555 Best of......................$19.95
Evanescence
00691186 Evanescence.............$22.99
Extreme
00690515 Pornograffitti............$24.99
John Fahey
00150257 Guitar Anthology $24.99
Tal Farlow
00125661 Best of......................$19.99
Five Finger Death Punch
00691009 5 Finger Death Punch $24.99
00691181 American Capitalism..$22.99
00128917 Wrong Side of Heaven & Righteous Side of Hell.$22.99
Fleetwood Mac
00690664 Best of......................$24.99
Flyleaf
00690870 Flyleaf......................$19.95
Foghat
00690986 Best of......................$22.99
Foo Fighters
00691024 Greatest Hits.............$24.99
00691115 Wasting Light............$24.99
Peter Frampton
00690842 Best of $22.99
Robben Ford
00690805 Best of......................$24.99
00120220 Guitar Anthology $29.99
Free
00694920 Best of......................$24.99
Rory Gallagher
00295410 Blues (Selections).....$24.99
Danny Gatton
00694807 88 Elmira St $24.99
Genesis
00690438 Guitar Anthology $24.99
Godsmack
00120167 Godsmack.................$19.95
00691048 The Oracle $22.99
Goo Goo Dolls
00690943 Greatest Hits Vol. 1....$24.99
Grateful Dead
00139460 Guitar Anthology $34.99

Green Day
00118259 ¡Tré! $21.99
00113073 ¡Uno! $21.99
Peter Green
00691190 Best of $24.99
Greta Van Fleet
00369065 The Battle at Garden's Gate $24.99
00287517 Anthem of the Peaceful Army $22.99
00287515 From the Fires...........$24.99
Patty Griffin
00690927 Children Running Through $19.95
Guns N' Roses
00690978 Chinese Democracy...$24.99
Buddy Guy
00691027 Anthology $24.99
00694854 Damn Right, I've Got the Blues............$19.95
Jim Hall
00690697 Best of......................$22.99
Ben Harper
00690840 Both Sides of the Gun .$19.95
00691018 Fight for Your Mind...$22.99
George Harrison
00694798 Anthology.................$24.99
Scott Henderson
00690841 Blues Guitar Collection$24.99
Jimi Hendrix
00692930 Are You Experienced?..$29.99
00692931 Axis: Bold As Love.....$24.99
00690304 Band of Gypsys..........$27.99
00690608 Blue Wild Angel.........$24.95
00275044 Both Sides of the Sky $22.99
00692932 Electric Ladyland.......$27.99
00690017 Live at Woodstock $29.99
00119619 People, Hell & Angels $27.99
00690602 Smash Hits $29.99
00691152 West Coast Seattle Boy (Anthology)........$29.99
00691332 Winterland $22.99
H.I.M.
00690843 Dark Light.................$19.95
Buddy Holly
00660029 Best of......................$24.99
John Lee Hooker
00690793 Anthology $29.99
Howlin' Wolf
00694905 Howlin' Wolf $22.99
Billy Idol
00690692 Very Best of..............$24.99
Imagine Dragons
00121961 Night Visions $22.99
Incubus
00690688 A Crow Left of the Murder.....................$19.95
Iron Maiden
00690790 Anthology.................$27.99
00691058 The Final Frontier $22.99
00200446 Guitar Tab $34.99
Alan Jackson
00690730 Guitar Collection.......$29.99
Elmore James
00694938 Master of the Electric Slide Guitar ..$19.99
Jane's Addiction
00690652 Best of......................$24.99
Jethro Tull
00690684 Aqualung..................$24.99
00690693 Guitar Anthology $24.99
00691182 Stand Up $22.99

John 5
00690898 The Devil Knows My Name $22.95
00690814 Songs for Sanity $19.95
00690751 Vertigo $19.95
Eric Johnson
00694912 Ah Via Musicom $24.99
00690660 Best of $29.99
00691076 Up Close $22.99
00690169 Venus Isle $29.99
Robert Johnson
00690271 New Transcriptions $27.99
Janis Joplin
00699131 Best of $24.99
Judas Priest
00690427 Best of $24.99
Kansas
00690277 Best of $24.99
Phil Keaggy
00690911 Best of $24.99
Toby Keith
00690727 Guitar Collection $19.99
The Killers
00690910 Sam's Town $19.95
Killswitch Engage
00120814 Disarm the Descent $22.99
Albert King
00690504 Very Best of $24.99
00124869 In Session $24.99
B.B. King
00690492 Anthology $29.99
00130447 Live at the Regal $19.99
00690444 Riding with the King $24.99
Freddie King
00690134 Collection $22.99
Marcus King
00327968 El Dorado $22.99
Kiss
00690157 Alive! $19.99
00690356 Alive II $24.99
00694903 Best of $29.99
00690355 Destroyer $19.99
00291163 Very Best of $24.99
Mark Knopfler
00690164 Guitar Styles $27.99
Greg Koch
00345767 Best of $29.99
Korn
00690780 Greatest Hits Vol. 1 $24.99
Kris Kristofferson
00690377 Collection $22.99
Lamb of God
00690834 Ashes of the Wake $24.99
00691187 Resolution $22.99
00690875 Sacrament $24.99
Ray LaMontagne
00690977 Gossip in the Grain $19.99
00691057 God Willin' & The Creek Don't Rise $22.99
John Lennon
00690679 Guitar Collection $27.99
Linkin Park
00690922 Minutes to Midnight $22.99
The Lumineers
00114563 The Lumineers $22.99
George Lynch
00690525 Best of $29.99
Lynyrd Skynyrd
00690955 All-Time Greatest Hits $24.99
00694954 New Best of $24.99
Yngwie Malmsteen
00690577 Anthology $29.99
Marilyn Manson
00690754 Lest We Forget $22.99
Bob Marley
00694956 Legend $22.99
00694945 Songs of Freedom $29.99
Pat Martino
00139168 Guitar Anthology $29.99
John McLaughlin
00129105 Guitar Tab Anthology $27.99
Mastodon
00690989 Crack the Skye $24.99
00236690 Emperor of Sand $22.99

00691176 The Hunter $24.99
00137718 Once More 'Round the Sun $24.99
Andy McKee
00691942 Art of Motion $24.99
00691034 Joyland $19.99
Don McLean
00120080 Songbook $22.99
Megadeth
00694952 Countdown to Extinction $24.99
00691015 Endgame $27.99
00276065 Greatest Hits $27.99
00694951 Rust in Peace $27.99
00690011 Youthanasia $24.99
John Mellencamp
00690505 Guitar Collection $24.99
Metallica
00209876 Hardwired... To Self-Destruct $24.99
Pat Metheny
00690562 Bright Size Life $24.99
00691073 Day Trip/ Tokyo Day Trip Live $22.99
00690646 One Quiet Night $24.99
00690559 Question & Answer $27.99
00690558 Trio 99-00 $24.99
00690561 Trio Live $27.99
00118836 Unity Band $22.99
00102590 What's It All About $24.99
Steve Miller Band
00690040 Young Hearts: Complete Greatest Hits $24.99
Ministry
00119338 Guitar Tab Collection $24.99
Wes Montgomery
00102591 Guitar Anthology $27.99
Gary Moore
00691092 Best of $27.99
00694802 Still Got the Blues $24.99
Alanis Morissette
00355456 Jagged Little Pill $22.99
Motion City Soundtrack
00691005 Best of $19.99
Mountain
00694958 Best of $22.99
Mumford & Sons
00691070 Sigh No More $22.99
Muse
00118196 The 2nd Law $19.99
00151195 Drones $19.99
My Morning Jacket
00690996 Collection $19.99
Matt Nathanson
00690984 Some Mad Hope $22.99
Night Ranger
00690883 Best of $19.99
Nirvana
00690611 Nirvana $24.99
00694895 Bleach $22.99
00694913 In Utero $22.99
00694883 Nevermind $19.99
00690026 Unplugged in New York $19.99
Nothing More
00265439 Guitar & Bass Tab Collection $24.99
The Offspring
00690807 Greatest Hits $24.99
Opeth
00243349 Best of $22.99
Roy Orbison
00691052 Black & White Night $22.99
Ozzy Osbourne
00694847 Best of $27.99
Brad Paisley
00690933 Best of $27.99
00690995 Play $29.99
Christopher Parkening
00690939 Solo Pieces $24.99
Les Paul
00690594 Best of $24.99
Pearl Jam
00694855 Ten $24.99
Periphery
00146043 Guitar Tab Collection $24.99

Carl Perkins
00690725 Best of $19.99
Tom Petty
00690499 Definitive Collection $24.99
Phish
00690176 Billy Breathes $24.99
Pink Floyd
00121933 Acoustic Collection $27.99
00690428 Dark Side of the Moon $22.99
00142677 The Endless River $19.99
00244637 Guitar Anthology $24.99
00239799 The Wall $27.99
Poison
00690789 Best of $22.99
Elvis Presley
00690299 King of Rock 'n' Roll $22.99
Prince
00690925 Very Best of $24.99
Queen
00690003 Classic Queen $24.99
00694975 Greatest Hits $27.99
Queens of the Stone Age
00254332 Villains $22.99
Queensryche
00690670 Very Best of $27.99
The Raconteurs
00690878 Broken Boy Soldiers $19.95
Radiohead
00109303 Guitar Anthology $29.99
Rage Against the Machine
00694910 Rage Against the Machine $24.99
00119834 Guitar Anthology $24.99
Rancid
00690179 And Out Come the Wolves $24.99
Ratt
00690426 Best of $24.99
Red Hot Chili Peppers
00690055 BloodSugarSexMagik $19.99
00690584 By the Way $24.99
00690379 Californication $22.99
00182634 The Getaway $24.99
00690673 Greatest Hits $24.99
00691166 I'm with You $22.99
00690255 Mother's Milk $24.99
00690090 One Hot Minute $22.95
00690852 Stadium Arcadium $29.99
00706518 Unlimited Loved $27.99
Jerry Reed
00694892 Guitar Style of $24.99
Django Reinhardt
00690511 Definitive Collection $24.99
Jimmie Rodgers
00690260 Guitar Collection $22.99
Rolling Stones
00690014 Exile on Main Street $24.99
00690631 Guitar Anthology $34.99
00694976 Some Girls $22.95
00690264 Tattoo You $19.95
Angelo Romero
00690974 Bella $19.99
David Lee Roth
00690685 Eat 'Em and Smile $24.99
00690942 Songs of Van Halen $19.95
Rush
00323854 The Spirit of Radio $22.99
Santana
00173534 Guitar Anthology $29.99
00690031 Greatest Hits $24.99
Joe Satriani
00276350 What Happens Next $24.99
Michael Schenker
00690796 Very Best of $24.99
Matt Schofield
00128870 Guitar Tab Collection $22.99
Scorpions
00690566 Best of $24.99
Bob Seger
00690604 Guitar Collection $24.99
Ed Sheeran
00234543 Divide $22.99
00138870 X $19.99

Kenny Wayne Shepherd
00690803 Best of $24.99
00151178 Ledbetter Heights $19.99
Shinedown
00692433 Amaryllis $22.99
Skillet
00122218 Rise $22.99
Slash
00691114 Guitar Anthology $34.99
Slayer
00690872 Christ Illusion $19.95
00690813 Guitar Collection $24.99
Slipknot
00690419 Slipknot $22.99
00690973 All Hope Is Gone $24.99
Smashing Pumpkins
00316982 Greatest Hits $24.99
Social Distortion
00690330 Live at the Roxy $24.99
Soundgarden
00690912 Guitar Anthology $24.99
Steely Dan
00120004 Best of $27.99
Steppenwolf
00694921 Best of $22.95
Mike Stern
00690655 Best of $27.99
Cat Stevens
14041588 Tea for the Tillerman $19.99
Rod Stewart
00690949 Guitar Anthology $19.99
Stone Temple Pilots
00322564 Thank You $26.99
Styx
00690520 Guitar Collection $22.99
Sublime
00120081 Sublime $22.99
00120122 40 oz. to Freedom $24.99
00690992 Robbin' the Hood $19.99
SUM 41
00690519 All Killer No Filler $19.95
00690929 Underclass Hero $19.95
Supertramp
00691072 Best of $24.99
Taylor Swift
00690994 Taylor Swift $22.99
00690993 Fearless $22.99
00115957 Red $21.99
00691063 Speak Now $22.99
System of a Down
00690531 Toxicity $19.99
James Taylor
00694824 Best of $22.99
Thin Lizzy
00694887 Best of $22.99
.38 Special
00690988 Guitar Anthology $22.99
Three Days Grace
00691039 Life Starts Now $22.99
Trans-Siberian Orchestra
00150209 Guitar Anthology $19.99
Merle Travis
00690233 Collection $24.99
Trivium
00253237 Guitar Tab Anthology $24.99
00123862 Vengeance Falls $24.99
Robin Trower
00690683 Bridge of Sighs $19.99
U2
00699191 Best of: 1980-1990 $24.99
00690732 Best of: 1990-2000 $29.99
00690894 18 Singles $27.99

Keith Urban
00124461 Guitar Anthology $29.99
Steve Vai
00690039 Alien Love Secrets $24.99
00690575 Alive in an Ultra World $22.95
00690172 Fire Garden $34.99
00156024 Guitar Anthology $39.99
00197570 Modern Primitive $29.99
00660137 Passion & Warfare $29.99
00690881 Real Illusions: Reflections $27.99
00690605 The Elusive Light and Sound, Vol. 1 $29.99
00694904 Sex and Religion $24.95
00110385 The Story of Light $24.99
00690392 The Ultra Zone $19.95
Van Halen
00700555 Van Halen $22.99
00295076 30 Classics $29.99
00700092 1984 $24.99
00700558 Fair Warning $24.99
Stevie Ray Vaughan
00690024 Couldn't Stand the Weather $22.99
00690116 Guitar Collection $29.99
00694879 In the Beginning $19.95
00660136 In Step $24.99
00660058 Lightnin' Blues 83-87 $29.99
00690550 Live at Montreux $29.99
00217455 Plays Slow Blues $24.99
00694835 The Sky Is Crying $24.99
00690025 Soul to Soul $19.95
00690015 Texas Flood $22.99
Volbeat
00109770 Guitar Collection $24.99
00121808 Outlaw Gentlemen & Shady Ladies $24.99
T-Bone Walker
00690132 Collection $22.99
Muddy Waters
00694789 Deep Blues $27.99
Doc Watson
00152161 Guitar Anthology $24.99
Weezer
00690071 The Blue Album $22.99
00691046 Rarities Edition $22.99
Paul Westerberg & The Replacements
00691036 Very Best of $19.99
The White Stripes
00237811 Greatest Hits $24.99
Whitesnake
00117511 Guitar Collection $24.99
The Who
00691941 Acoustic Guitar Collection $22.99
00690447 Best of $24.99
Wilco
00691006 Guitar Collection $24.99
The Yardbirds
00690596 Best of $24.99
Yes
00122303 Guitar Collection $24.99
Dwight Yoakam
00690916 Best of $22.99
Frank Zappa
00690507 Apostrophe $22.99
00690443 Hot Rats $22.99
00690624 One Size Fits All $27.99
00690623 Over-Nite Sensation $24.99
ZZ Top
00121684 Early Classics $27.99
00690589 Guitar Anthology $27.99
00690960 Guitar Classics $24.99

HAL•LEONARD®
Complete songlists and more at **www.halleonard.com**
Prices and availability subject to change without notice.

How To...

This series gives musicians the skinny on a wide variety of topics. Written by different authors with specific expertise, each title delves deep into the subject, getting readers started on the skills they're most interested in.

GUITAR BOOKS

How to Build Guitar Chops
by Chad Johnson
00147679 Book/Online Audio $16.99

How to Enjoy Guitar with Just 3 Chords
by David Harrison
00288990 Book Only..$7.99

How to Fingerpick Songs on Guitar
by Chad Johnson
00155364 Book/Online Video.................................$14.99

How to Get Better at Guitar
by Thorsten Kober
00157666 Book/Online Audio $19.99

How to Play Blues-Fusion Guitar
by Joe Charupakorn
00137813 Book/Online Audio $19.99

How to Play Blues/Rock Guitar Solos
by David Grissom
00249561 Book/Online Audio $16.99

How to Play Boogie Woogie Guitar
by Dave Rubin
00157974 Book/Online Video.................................$14.99

How to Play Country Lead Guitar
by Jeff Adams
00131103 Book/Online Audio $19.99

How to Play Outside Guitar Licks
by Chris Buono
00140855 Book/Online Video.................................$19.99

How to Play Rock Lead Guitar
by Brooke St. James
00146260 Book/Online Video.................................$14.99

How to Play Rock Rhythm Guitar
by Brooke St. James
00146261 Book/Online Video.................................$14.99

How to Strum Chords on Guitar
by Burgess Speed
00154902 Book/Online Video.................................$14.99

BASS BOOKS

How to Create Rock Bass Lines
by Steve Gorenberg
00151784 Book/Online Audio $16.99

How to Play Blues Bass
by Mark Epstein
00260179 Book/Online Audio $14.99

DRUM BOOKS

How to Build Drum Grooves Over Bass Lines
by Alan Arber
00287564 Book/Online Audio $16.99

How to Play Rock Drums
by David Lewitt
00138541 Book/Online Audio $16.99

PIANO/KEYBOARD BOOKS

How to Play Blues Piano by Ear
by Todd Lowry
00121704 Book/Online Audio $16.99

How to Play Boogie Woogie Piano
by Arthur Migliazza & Dave Rubin
00140698 Book/Online Audio $16.99

How to Play R&B Soul Keyboards
by Henry Brewer
00232890 Book/Online Audio $16.99

How to Play Solo Jazz Piano
by John Valerio
00147731 Book/Online Audio $16.99

STRINGS BOOK

How to Play Contemporary Strings
by Julie Lyonn Lieberman
00151259 Book/Online Media................................$16.99

UKULELE BOOK

How to Play Solo Ukulele
by Chad Johnson
00159809 Book/Online Audio $16.99

VOCAL BOOK

How to Sight Sing
by Chad Johnson
00156132 Book/Online Audio $16.99

OTHER VOLUMES

How to Improvise Over Chord Changes
by Shawn Wallace, Dr. Keith Newton,
Kris Johnson & Steve Kortyka
00138009 Book Only...$24.99

How to Read Music
by Mark Phillips
00137870 Book Only...$9.99

How to Record at Home on a Budget
by Chad Johnson
00131211 Book/Online Audio $19.99

How to Write Your First Song
by Dave Walker
00138010 Book/Online Audio $16.99

HAL•LEONARD®
www.halleonard.com

Prices and availability subject to change without notice.

Dynamic Drum Publications from Berklee Press

BOOKS

BERKLEE INSTANT DRUM SET
by Ron Savage
This book/CD pack teaches first-time drummers rock, funk, and jazz beats within minutes. Features an accompanying CD so you can jam with the band in a variety of musical styles.
50449513 Book/CD Pack $17.99

BERKLEE PRACTICE METHOD: DRUM SET
by Ron Savage, Casey Scheuerell and the Berklee Faculty
This sensational series lets you improve your intuitive sense of timing and improvisation, develop your technique and reading ability, and master your role in the groove.
50449429 Book/CD Pack $14.95

BEYOND THE BACKBEAT:
FROM ROCK & FUNK TO JAZZ & LATIN
by Larry Finn
Learn how to take any basic rock/funk drum beat and morph it into jazz and world music feels. Improve your chops, expand your versatility, and develop your own style.
50449447 Book/CD Pack $19.95

DOUBLE-BASS DRUM INTEGRATION
These timetables and other road-tested exercises methodically introduce double pedal patterns into your beats, helping you play them intuitively, revealing the possibilities of double bass drums.
00120208 Book/Online Audio $19.99

DRUM SET WARM-UPS
by Rod Morgenstein
Legendary drummer Rod Morgenstein reveals his innovative warm-up method designed to limber up your entire body.
50449465 Book $12.99

DRUM STUDIES
by Dave Vose
These studies will help you to master a broad range of techniques and integrate them into your playing so that you can achieve greater depth in your grooves and general precision in all your drumming.
50449617 Book.. $12.99

THE READING DRUMMER – SECOND EDITION
by Dave Vose
Features: more than 50 lessons complete with general practice tips; steady learning progression from reading quarter notes to 16th-note triplets; and more.
50449458 Book $14.99

LEARNING TO LISTEN:
THE JAZZ JOURNEY OF GARY BURTON
by Gary Burton
Gary Burton shares his 50 years of experiences at the top of the jazz scene.
00117798 Book.. $27.99

MASTERING THE ART OF BRUSHES
by Jon Hazilla
This in-depth workshop, complete with helpful diagrams practice audio, features 10 essential concepts, 32 brush patterns, rhythm table exercises, and more.
50449459 Book/Online Audio $19.99

PHRASING: ADVANCED RUDIMENTS FOR
CREATIVE DRUMMING
by Russ Gold
Phrasing will help you expand your vocabulary using standard rudiments and exciting rhythmic concepts, making your playing more conversational, dynamic, and focused.
00120209 Book... $19.99

EIGHT ESSENTIALS OF DRUMMING
by Ron Savage
Become a well-rounded drummer with sound technique, solid time, and expressive musicianship by mastering these eight essentials.
50448048 Book/CD Pack $19.99

READING STUDIES FOR DRUMS AND PERCUSSION
by Ron Delp
These exercises will help musicians move between instruments more accurately, while enhancing their reading ability for recording work, shows, and the theater pit.
50449550 Book $9.99

RUDIMENT GROOVES FOR DRUM SET
by Rick Considine
Discover how rudiments become the foundation for all grooves and moves, including: single and double strokes; stroked rolls; drags; flams; and more.
50448001 Book/Online Audio $19.95

STICKINGS & ORCHESTRATIONS FOR DRUM SET
by Casey Scheuerell
Technical explanations and extensive practice exercises with the play-along audio will help you make your fills become more vibrant and your solos more virtuosic.
50448049 Book/Online Audio $22.99

WORLD JAZZ DRUMMING
by Mark Walker
This book/CD pack teaches you how to: incorporate world instruments into a standard drum kit; coordinate stick, foot, hand techniques to enrich your palette of articulations; and more.
50449568 Book/CD Pack $22.99

DVDs

BASIC AFRO-CUBAN RHYTHMS FOR
DRUM SET AND HAND PERCUSSION
featuring Ricardo Monzón
Learn how to play and practice the classic rhythms of the Afro-Cuban tradition with Berklee professor Ricardo Monzón. 55 minutes.
50448012 DVD $19.95

BEGINNING DJEMBE
by Michael Markus & Joe Galeota
This hands-on workshop will help you produce a good sound, develop a healthy playing technique, and learn the essential concepts and rhythms of West African djembe drumming. 1 hr., 36 minutes
50449639 DVD $14.99

CREATIVE JAZZ IMPROVISATION
FOR DRUM SET
Featuring Yoron Israel
Yoron Israel will help you to enhance your improvisational language and lead you to more musical, concise and dynamic drum set solos and comping. 51 minutes.
50449549 DVD $24.95

KENWOOD DENNARD:
THE STUDIO/TOURING DRUMMER
Dennard teaches how to: get the most out of every practice session, internalize the melody, play melodic solos, and more! 61 minutes.
50448034 DVD $19.95

NEW WORLD DRUMMING
by Pablo Peña "Pablitodrum"
Learn to: Play drum set in a percussion ensemble, incorporate world rhythms and sounds into a standard drum kit, create drum parts that are appropriate to the style and ensemble, and more. 41 minutes.
50449547 DVD $24.95

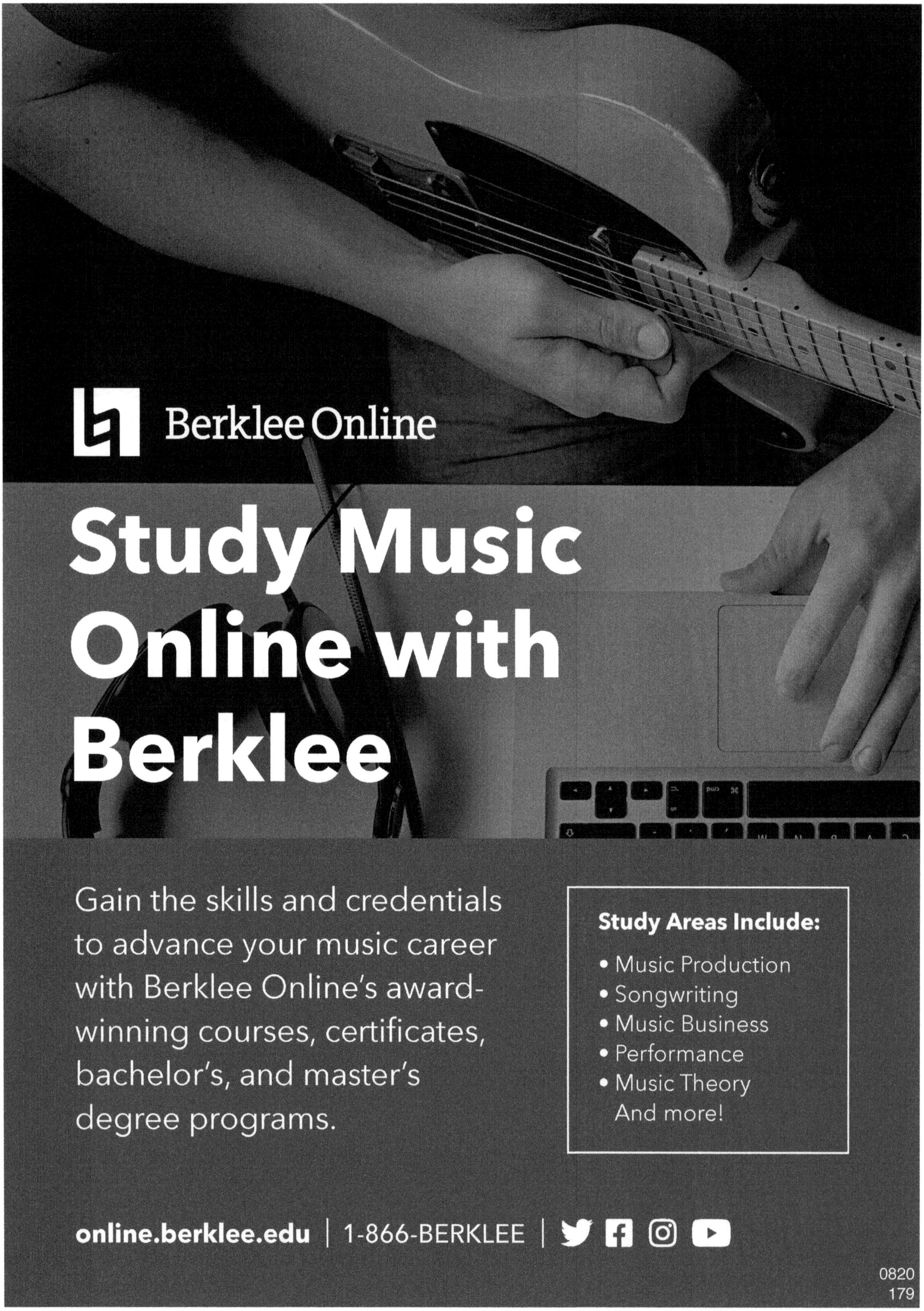
Berklee Online
Study Music Online with Berklee
Gain the skills and credentials to advance your music career with Berklee Online's award-winning courses, certificates, bachelor's, and master's degree programs.
Study Areas Include:
• Music Production
• Songwriting
• Music Business
• Performance
• Music Theory
And more!
online.berklee.edu | 1-866-BERKLEE |
0820
179